CAMBRIDGE LIBRARY COLLECTION

Books of enduring scholarly value

Egyptology

The large-scale scientific investigation of Egyptian antiquities by Western scholars began as an unintended consequence of Napoleon's invasion of Egypt during which, in 1799, the Rosetta Stone was discovered. The military expedition was accompanied by French scholars, whose reports prompted a wave of enthusiasm that swept across Europe and North America resulting in the Egyptian Revival style in art and architecture. Increasing numbers of tourists visited Egypt, eager to see the marvels being revealed by archaeological excavation. Writers and booksellers responded to this growing interest with publications ranging from technical site reports to tourist guidebooks and from children's histories to theories identifying the pyramids as repositories of esoteric knowledge. This series reissues a wide selection of such books. They reveal the gradual change from the 'tomb-robbing' approach of early excavators to the highly organised and systematic approach of Flinders Petrie, the 'father of Egyptology', and include early accounts of the decipherment of the hieroglyphic script.

Ancient Gaza

A pioneering Egyptologist, Sir William Matthew Flinders Petrie (1853–1942) excavated over fifty sites and trained a generation of archaeologists. Now reissued in two volumes are the four excavation reports, published between 1931 and 1934, covering his extensive dig at Tell el-Ajjul in Palestine. The reports scrupulously record the finds of artefacts dating from the Copper Age and extending to the Hyksos period. Descriptions of the working party's struggles against malaria and the elements highlight Petrie's devotion to his work. Volume 1 combines the first two reports, first published in 1931 and 1932, and includes descriptions of various cemeteries, tombs, palaces and horse burials. Each report features a section of photographs and sketches of tombs, pottery, weapons and jewellery. Petrie wrote prolifically throughout his long career, and a great many of his Egyptological publications – for both specialists and non-specialists – are also reissued in this series.

T0381731

Cambridge University Press has long been a pioneer in the reissuing of out-of-print titles from its own backlist, producing digital reprints of books that are still sought after by scholars and students but could not be reprinted economically using traditional technology. The Cambridge Library Collection extends this activity to a wider range of books which are still of importance to researchers and professionals, either for the source material they contain, or as landmarks in the history of their academic discipline.

Drawing from the world-renowned collections in the Cambridge University Library and other partner libraries, and guided by the advice of experts in each subject area, Cambridge University Press is using state-of-the-art scanning machines in its own Printing House to capture the content of each book selected for inclusion. The files are processed to give a consistently clear, crisp image, and the books finished to the high quality standard for which the Press is recognised around the world. The latest print-on-demand technology ensures that the books will remain available indefinitely, and that orders for single or multiple copies can quickly be supplied.

The Cambridge Library Collection brings back to life books of enduring scholarly value (including out-of-copyright works originally issued by other publishers) across a wide range of disciplines in the humanities and social sciences and in science and technology.

Ancient Gaza

Volume 1

W.M. Flinders Petrie

CAMBRIDGE
UNIVERSITY PRESS

University Printing House, Cambridge, CB2 8BS, United Kingdom

Published in the United States of America by Cambridge University Press, New York

Cambridge University Press is part of the University of Cambridge.
It furthers the University's mission by disseminating knowledge in the pursuit of
education, learning and research at the highest international levels of excellence.

www.cambridge.org
Information on this title: www.cambridge.org/9781108066082

This edition first published 1931 and 1932
This digitally printed version 2013

ISBN 978-1-108-06608-2 Paperback

BRITISH SCHOOL OF ARCHAEOLOGY IN EGYPT
AIDED BY NEW YORK UNIVERSITY

ANCIENT GAZA
I
TELL EL AJJŪL

BY

FLINDERS PETRIE, Kt., F.R.S., F.B.A.

LONDON
BRITISH SCHOOL OF ARCHAEOLOGY IN EGYPT
UNIVERSITY COLLEGE, GOWER ST., W.C.1
AND
BERNARD QUARITCH
11 GRAFTON ST., NEW BOND ST., W.1
1931

PRINTED IN GREAT BRITAIN
BY HAZELL, WATSON AND VINEY, LTD.
LONDON AND AYLESBURY

BRITISH SCHOOL OF ARCHAEOLOGY IN EGYPT

CONTENTS

LIST OF PLATES

ANCIENT GAZA

INTRODUCTION

1. THE site of Tell el Ajjūl lies about four miles south-west of modern Gaza, on the edge of the Wady Ghazzeh, and near the high road which has led, all through the ages, from Africa into Asia. I had visited it and seen that it was of the Bronze Age, before we went to Gerar in 1926, but the extent of it was not realised till Mr. Starkey went over it in 1930. Preparations were then made, and some rooms built for our camp, before leaving Beth-pelet. These were occupied in October by some of our staff, only to find that malaria was rampant at that time of year, and at the beginning of the work more than a quarter of our labourers were in hospital in consequence. The rest of our staff had in November to turn off elsewhere, and to do more clearance of the Ramesside cemetery in the great fosse at Bethpelet.

2. It was not, then, till 17th December, 1930, that we could all reside at Tell el Ajjūl, and the work was carried on there till the latter part of April, 1931. The party consisted of Mr. R. Richmond Brown, Mr. and Mrs. H. D. Colt, Mr. L. Harding, Dr. G. Parker, Professor and Lady Petrie, Mr. G. F. Royds, Mr. N. Scott, Mr. and Mrs. J. L. Starkey, Miss O. Tufnell, and Mr. J. G. Vernon. In particular we thank the professional help of Dr. Parker, who attended to the health of all the workers, and Mr. Royds, who did much of the surveying. Some of the photographs are due to the skill of Mr. Brown.

3. The malaria was so serious a hindrance, and had so depopulated this part of the country, that in March we appealed to the Department of Public Health. The valley was officially inspected by the malaria expert, and under our direction our men cut two and a half miles of canal, and filled up the pools. So far, this seems to have been effective in prevention, but the reclamation and benefit of all this region is not a matter which the Government should devolve on private enterprise, and it is hoped that the expenses of this needful service to the country will be returned.

The dating used in this volume is that which results from all the Egyptian sources, as fully stated in *Ancient Egypt*, 1929, p. 33, and 1931, p. 1. All other dating repudiates a part of the recorded material.

According to this latest revision of the dating, the XIIth dynasty ranged from 2584 to 2371 B.C. The XIIIth Egyptian dynasty lasted till 1918, XIVth till 1734, XVIIth till 1583. The Hyksos at the same time ruled in the Delta : XVth dynasty, 2371 till 2111, and XVIth till 1593.

CHAPTER I

THE HISTORICAL POSITION

4. BEFORE describing any details, it is well to outline the conditions of the site and the successive periods examined, in order to state the fixed points of dating.

The sand-dune region between the Tell and the coast is largely covered with Byzantine and early Arab pottery, which is seen at all the bare intervals between the dunes. Though we did not work there, much was brought up to us by the children during the short days of work in Ramadan. The periods of the finds were widely varied. On pl. xviii are a Hyksos toggle-pin (about 2000 B.C.), two fibulae with hand clutch (600 B.C.), Scythian triangular arrow heads of the same age, a disc from a finger-ring with the shield pattern of the Macedonians (100 B.C.), and dozens of finger-rings of later design (A.D. 400 to 1000 ?). The copper pins were mostly made with coiled heads, but many bore cubes with truncated corners. All of the copper and bronze here is in a peculiar condition, uncorroded but covered with a thin black patina. The metal remains quite flexible, even in the thinnest pins. This black coating on copper, formed close to the sea-coast, and exposed to the air for centuries, seems to be probably the oxychloride of copper. Great quantities of pins, over four thousand, were gradually collected, and also very debased coins of early Arab style.

The whole region for miles seems to have been widely occupied, without leaving any mounds or ruins. Large quantities of early Arab coloured glazes were found, and all handed over to Mr. Richmond, Director of the Antiquity Department, for study.

A statue of Serapis, usually referred to Tell el Ajjūl (COOK, *Relig. Anc. Pal.*, p. 181) was actually discovered at Tell es Sanam, a small mound of Roman age, on the south side of the wady, near the coast. It was removed to Constantinople.

5. The site of Tell el Ajjūl. The general view from the top is on pl. ii. The valley of the Wady Ghazzeh spreads out here to 1,000 ft. wide, with a stream-bed along the northern side ; when in flood the whole wady is filled. The sea is about a mile and a half from the Tell, and, on turning to look inland, one sees the Red House, so familiar in the War, a mile away in the opposite direction. The valley is an estuary silted up, for the natural valley is one-fifth as wide at a mile or two farther. The sea coming in so far would make this a port for small vessels, and there was none better between Egypt and Haifa.

6. For the outline of the city, see pl. lii. It stands on a sandstone hill, at the north side of the stream, and was thus defended, so that no fortification was made on the stream face, except scarping the hill. The stream itself formed the ditch on this side. The sandstone is a mass of ancient dunes, solidified by gypsum working up from below the soil, owing to long drought each summer. This gypsum forms nodules in the sand, and similar nodules are formed inside pottery within four thousand years. The nodules also occur in the marl over the sand.

The river face of the hill is shown in pl. ii, 2, broken down by weathering and quarrying. The natural slope of the Tell is seen in ii, 3, at the north corner, smothered with a couple of feet of sand blown over it. The fig trees have been planted in the last few years.

7. On the plan of the Tell, pl. lii, it is clear how largely it has been eaten out by denudation at the sides. It is, however, only in the deepest cutting of the hollows that the sandstone is reached, and the rest of the scoop is cut through the ruins. The north corner is the highest part, and thence westward it has been recently planted with fig trees. The rest of the Tell is regularly ploughed. As it was

proclaimed as an ancient site, the cultivators are only tolerated, and any part can legally be excavated.

All that was dug this year was at the south corner, where a convenient ravine could be filled up level, and so compensate the cultivator with more land. Some digging was also done at the north-east gate. The Government survey marks are lettered by us from A to F on pl. lii. Our hutting is at the east corner.

8. Along the east and south-east sides we trenched to find the fosse, and the vertical outer side is marked by a border-line on liii. From that line the slope extended upward to the inner edge, which was the crest of the Tell. The whole of the upper part had been stripped by denudation, removing any city wall. There is no trace of a fosse on the south-west side, where the estuary supplied defence ; but it doubtless extends on the north and north-west, heaped over with blown sand, so that we have not sought for it.

The old ground level outside of the fosse on the south-east side is covered with about 5 ft. of silt. The bottom of the fosse has not yet been reached, but it is probably 25 ft. below the outside, and 85 ft. below the inside. The slope up was about 150 ft. long at 34°. Fuller details will be given by future work (see sect. 51).

The comparative areas within ancient cities in Palestine were, in acres, Lachish 1 (Troy 2, Mykenae 3), Sandehanna 4, Jedideh 5, Zakarieh 9, Ophel 11, Taanak 12, Megiddo 12, Safy 20, Gezer 22, Ajjūl 33.

9. On excavating the south corner, the tops of the walls showed at only a foot or two down in some parts. In three of the chambers thus opened there were scarabs of Apepa I, the great Hyksos king, of about 2250 B.C. (pls. xiii, xiv, 3, 44, 143). These give a date for the latest buildings. No later occupation was found, except a few little patches of Roman and Arab pottery, and some xviiith dyn. shards. In the valley below were some graves of the early xviiith dyn., but so far, the dwellings of that time have not appeared.

10. Proceeding to earlier times, we must distinguish between the nomadic Hyksos and the Canaanites, whom they overran. The Hyksos in Palestine used the pottery of the period of the xiith dyn., as dated at Byblos, and daggers of Cyprus and of Crete. In Egypt their tombs have Egyptian and North Syrian pottery. They do not seem to have had any distinctive civilisation, nor any peculiar

object unless it be a recurved knife (xvii, 35), which is also found in their graves in Egypt (*Hyksos and Isr. Cities*, vi, 9). Even this may very likely be Cretan (see *Tools and W.*, xxv, 79). Without any distinctive belongings, they seem to have been nomads, using skin and wood vessels.

It is not therefore to the Hyksos that we must attribute the regularly built city and the fine and varied pottery : all this belonged to the Canaanite civilisation, which was overlaid by the Hyksos rule, like the Levantine ruled by the nomadic Turk.

11. In the cemeteries we likewise see the distinction. The burials with horses obviously belong to the Hyksos, who introduced the horse to the West. Such burials are always extended at length, regularly composed. Other graves with similar pottery, both here and at Beth-pelet, have no horses, and the bodies are contorted, with the limbs irregularly spread, as if stiffened at death. They must, then, be those of Canaanites.

12. In the part of the city immediately below the Hyksos houses there is a burnt layer, at 726–44 ins. level. This may be due to the Hyksos conquest, or rather perhaps to the raid of Senusert III, when he reached Shechem, 2460 B.C. Below this are other buildings and pottery of Canaanite type, with scarabs of the xiith dyn., and others of the so-called Hyksos types. Now, as there are no industrial

13. In all this age of Canaanites and Hyksos, there has not appeared a single example of the button-badge, which distinguished the Syrians who formed the viith and viiith dyns. of Egypt. Such badges are known from Cilicia, Aleppo, and Bismiya in Mesopotamia. We can only conclude that the people who used them did not settle at the Wady Ghazzeh, but must have swept away any inhabitants there in the course of their conquest of Egypt. They are represented at Ajjūl by an era of desolation.

This desolation period is marked by the denudation cutting away about 8 ft. of soil, as we shall next notice, and thus leaving the old door slabs standing isolated, when the tombs to which they belonged had been entirely washed away. All this implies a long period of neglect, and this was doubtless due to the attention of the conquerors being fixed on the wealth of Egypt.

14. Next before this movement there was a Copper Age civilisation. The many objects of this period were dated best by a string of large carnelian beads. These are not so finely formed, or so translucent, as those of the vth dyn., but they are much better than others at the close of the vith (see block). This fairly places them early in the vith dyn., about 3300 B.C. The beads were associated with pottery of a sort never found in the Canaanite or Hyksos

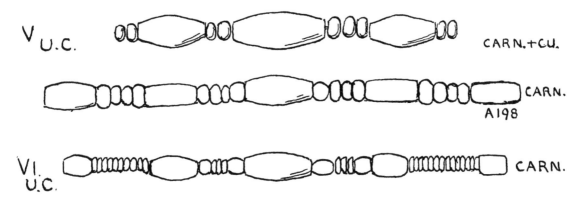

products of the Hyksos, it is very unlikely that they started scarabs in imitation of Egypt. It seems far more probable that all the so-called Hyksos scarabs were of Canaanite work, made before and during Hyksos rule. The term Canaanite is used here, as it is expressly said, in various places in the Old Testament, that those people occupied the coast-lands, while the Amorite was in the hill-country. So the best we can do is to name people of 2500 B.C. according to the records of 1200.

periods. The main type is the large ovate jar with flat base (xxvi. 1, 2, with 5, 6, 8), accompanied by flat-based bowls and cylindrical cups. All of this pottery is weakly baked, a pale drab ware, never reddened by strong heat. With such pottery were copper weapons, distinguished by their condition of slight surface change, without any split or lumpy oxidation. The rapier (xviii, 1), the dagger with skew handle (without pottery, but adjacent tombs of Copper Age), and the remarkable spear-daggers (xix, 5, 6) which by the recurved tang were fitted with handles—all of these are unlike any weapons of later times. The large ovate pots sometimes have the slight vestige of a wavy ledge handle, linking them to the Neolithic.

15. The tombs of this age, in their best type, have square entrance shafts about 8 or 10 ft. deep; a thick slab of limestone (xi, 1), covers the doorway (xi, 2) of a domed rock chamber. In relation to these, the tombs at Gezer, called Canaanite, have circular entrance pits, and not square as above.

It is some of these tombs which have been entirely swept away by denudation (xi, 3). In the foreground is one door slab, A; beyond that another square door slab, B, with the floor of the tomb and a jar lying exposed. All of the earth around these slabs was loose silt and, after the denudation of the marl tomb, the slabs had been left standing in the open. In the flooding and desolation there was no man about to overthrow them, or to utilise them, though such large slabs were scarce.

16. The type of these tombs is most like that of the iiird to vth dyns. in Egypt, as at Bashkatib, Meydum, and elsewhere. From this, and the beads, the Copper Age in Palestine may well be equated with the Copper Age of the Old Kingdom in Egypt. Probably this civilisation perished in the middle of the vith dyn., when the owners of the button-badges began to appear in Egypt. Not a single detail of the tombs or objects of this civilisation survived into the Canaanite period of the Egyptian Middle Kingdom. For the works of the Copper Age, see Chapter VI.

The settlements of the preceding age, the Neolithic, do not occur at Ajjūl, but have been found in the neighbourhood at Beth-pelet; these have been studied, and placed in order, by Mr. Macdonald in his work with us last year, and are being published in *Beth-pelet* ii.

CHAPTER II

THE HYKSOS PERIOD

17. The Hyksos invaders intruded on the Canaanite civilisation; the only really distinctive remains of that people are the burials with horses, and pit tombs with loculi. Many other burials may be of the same race, but not distinguishable from the Canaanite burials. The destruction of the bones by ancient plunderers and by decay often prevents the distinction being drawn from the attitude of the skeletons.

The best example of horse burial is in tomb 411. The plan is in pl. lvii. Evidently of the same class are the other tombs, 246, 407, 406, 263 on the same plate, 210 on pl. ix, 247 and 445 not drawn (see vii). The views of 210 and 411 are on viii, and of 263 and 407 on x. The heads were laid in any direction, and in five instances there are two bodies in one loculus, always feet to feet. These suggest a custom of wife burial, but in 407 a multiple burial seems clearly due to pestilence, as a man had a boy within his arm, and a woman had another child. Perhaps, then, all multiple burials were due to pestilence. The bodies were always laid full length, and usually composed regularly. Sometimes the legs were bent, as 407 (x, 3).

18. What the upper part of these tombs may have been is a difficult question. They were evidently family tombs, from the number of bodies together. There was no trace of fallen roof in the pits; had they been originally domed, no denudation could have prevented most of the roof falling in, yet the filling was ordinary silt. There was never any trace of a central pillar to support a timber or brushwood roof. Yet if the tomb were filled up with earth, it would be an awkward matter to dig down and clear part of the side for additional loculi.

19. The total of types of pottery in these graves is as follows: 6 N 8; 18 K 1"; 23 E 1, 4; 23 J 7; 34 B⁷, ⁸; 35 P 4, 6; 35 Q; 38 B², ³; 38 C 2; 38 G 4; 38 N ¹, ⁴; 38 O ⁶; 38 P 4; 43 D 4, 6; 43 E, E 4; 43 F 3; 51 B 6; 51 G 4"; 51 G 11; 60 H 9, 13; 60 Q 3, 3"; 74 O, O 3, 3', 3", O 5, O 11, O 13; 89 A; 91 A 1. These types seem to extend over all the early and middle Hyksos age.

The toggle-pin is usual, and scarabs are found in most of the tombs.

20. Burials of asses are also found, as tomb 101, (see viii, 5, 6, and ix). These four asses were sacrificed and placed at a rather higher level than the human burial.

Another remarkable burial is a large mass of bones, dissevered, placed nearer the mouth of the tunnel, 590 (see pl. vii, 2). This mass of bones has been left for an anatomist to separate; I observed a large horse skull, also ass, gazelle, ox, and human bones. The human skulls were apart from vertebrae; an arm was complete from fingers to ball of the humerus, but without scapula. A leg of an ass was similarly dissevered. The fine horse burial, 411, had only one leg in place ; three had been removed, the hinder-legs by chopping away the sides of the pelvis. This custom of removing limbs needs further examples, and comparisons from other lands, before we can know its meaning.

A late Hyksos burial in the lower city had elaborate strings of ostrich shell beads, forming a chest ornament ; the position on the body is seen in vii, 3 ; a larger view of a group behind the back is in vi, 4.

CHAPTER III

THE CANAANITE PERIOD

21. It may be an assumption to call this age Canaanite, as the earliest localisation of the name, linked with Gaza (Jud. i. 18), and with the sea (Num. xiii. 29), is nearly a thousand years later than the city with which we are dealing. Yet we do not know of any change of population between the periods, except the Egyptian invasion which scarcely altered the inhabitants.

The distinctive feature in the burials is the random position of the limbs, apparently due to burying the body as it stiffened in death. This is seen in pl. x, 406, and in the well-preserved tomb 550 at Beth-pelet, pl. xvii. The latter is absolutely of the Hyksos period, as eight types of the pottery are identical, and five others closely like those in the city at Ajjūl. The forms of the tombs at Beth-pelet were bilobate (Bp. xvii, xviii), but here no such tombs have been found. The most usual type is simply a circular pit, and half as often a long grave ; only rarely is there a square pit. The period of all of these is fixed by the types of pottery, contemporary with the Hyksos. A remarkable tomb was lined with rough stones (xi, 5), like one at Gezer, and fallen into it were parts of a cement slab, with fine facing, which had apparently covered it to about 5 ft. across. Also a cubical block of sandstone (xi, 6, xxxvi) faced with stucco ; a hole vertically through it seems intended to hold a staff or standard of some kind. This is the only surface monument of the Bronze Age known (Jerusalem Mus.). Other burials of the late Hyksos type are found inserted in the city houses and grain pits ; but all their types are later than those in the houses, of xvith or xviith dynasty.

22. The buildings, so far as excavated in about a fiftieth of the city, are of excellent construction ; the bricks are of a hard yellow clay, and of large size, up

to twelve times the bulk of a modern brick. Often they are laid as headers extending through a 22-in. wall. The clay mortar is so strong that a lintel of a door is formed of only two bricks held up by the setting (see pl. i, frontispiece. This is between rooms J and D, pl. liii). The general appearance of the ruins is given on pl. iii. Each view has a letter at the margin A–E, repeated at the identical point in the next view. This forms a panorama taken from station B in the plan, pl. liv. A–C are in the later part at a higher level, C–E are in the earlier part at a lower level. In iii, 1 and 2, is seen a long wall facing a street ; this street runs on to the right hand until the clearance stops blankly at the unopened ground. From that point is taken the street view iv, 1, looking back along this street. A little to the left of the street is the highest part remaining of the uncleared ground. That is around survey mark B, of which the staff is visible; from that point the panorama, iii, was taken.

In iv, 1, the street line has not yet been cleared to the bottom, but only a little below an old level, at which a drain was made in the middle of the road. The brick lining of the square drain is left standing up. In iv, 2, 3, the successive rooms of the main house are shown, looking south-west from room A M, and north-east from J.

23. The general plan of the south corner of the Tell is given on pl. liii. The rooms are necessarily lettered in the order in which they were cleared out. The numbers over 500 are the level in inches above sea of the top and base of the walls, or the ground surface. The numbers under 100 are those of burials. The wady side runs along the upper margin. A row of buildings bordered it, with a street from point B northward. A main road branched from that running east, as in iii, 1. The solid black walling is that above the burnt level, xvth dyn., the dotted lines are later additions ; the open outlines to the left are below the burnt level, of the xiith dyn. At the north-east end are many grain pits sunk in the sandstone, the stores of the xiith dyn. Burials of the xiith dyn. were made in them, including that of Hor-ka. Later burials disturbed these, and walls of houses were run across the old graveyard. The old dune sandstone here is about 750 level, and slopes down to the left hand to 583.

The main house is a square block, A, AB, H, J ; this opened into an annex from J to D, Y, C (door in i ; hearth in C, vi, 2). This house was altered later, and a cattle trough built above the hearth room. The entrance was up the lane AA into room A, so much broken down that it is obliterated. The burial between G and J was inserted after the place was abandoned.

24. The lane AA led also to a shrine at AF. The plan of this is added below on double scale. Referring to the level numbers, the worshipper stepped up from the ground 261 level on to the step, 768. Here he could wash his feet on the bench of shells, 780 (see v, 2). The water ran down into a drain pit lined with stone, 765. From the clean shell platform he stepped on to the clean white stucco floor, and so passed into the lobby, which had successive raised flooring from 761 to 768. Thence he passed to the shrine, floored with plaster at 760. This is best seen in the view looking back to the entrance, v, 1. The connection with the plan is given by the corresponding levels on the view. The sides of the shrine were white plastered, without any paintings or ornament. None of the common pottery figures of gods were found, nor any place for a statue. It was as bare, simple, puritanical, as the most fervent Wahaby could wish. Is this a primitive cult of North-West Arabia, which was adopted by Judaism and Islam? The ablutions before prayer were likewise provided at Serabit (*Researches in Sinai*, 105) before the Law at the Exodus.

25. Nor is this shrine alone, but a smaller shrine is seen towards the south. Outside this was a more elaborate shell bench (xii, 6) with a central drain. This led into a large jar beneath, which was disclosed by our excavation (xii, 5). The under-cutting was done preparatory to removing the bench in sections. These were built together and shown in our July exhibition.

26. At the top of the plan is an oblong kiln, the floor of which is at 666. The view from the south end, looking towards the draught hole, is in vi, 5. The supports were very large bricks, set on end. The plan is given in pl. lii. Along the best preserved side were four flue holes, at 28 ins. over the floor, rising 20 ins. to the remaining top of the wall. The spring of the entry arch remained, but the whole of the table for the pottery was decayed (see sect. 49).

In the lower level, at the left on liii, is a circular kiln, in room DF. This had the pierced table for the pottery (vi, 3); below that was brick corbelling to support the table over the furnace (vi, 4). The same form of kiln is now used in the potteries at Gaza. The date of this kiln must, however, be before the

building of the rooms of the xiith dyn., as they would block the wind from the draught hole. Another circular kiln, much damaged, is to the west of this in DK. It has been emptied, to far below the walls around, so it is also older than the buildings. The wasters from these kilns have not yet been found.

27. In the same region are two privies. One in DK is given in vii, 5. The hole in the seat opens into a pit about 6 ft. deep lined with rough stone. At the doorway in the plan is drawn a thin wall; this is part of an earlier building, at a lower level. The whole chamber is 112 × 50 in. Far west at DP is another privy, which had a large jar below it.

28. Besides the fire hearth in the large hall, C, vi, 2, there was another south of that at the limit of the present work, at level 756, shown on vi, 1.

In the room X was a bath; the inner end, for a length of about 8 ft., was about 3 ft. below the outer end; the whole surfaces were covered with white plaster. Another bath lay between this and the small shrine; about a foot height of the walls remained, and that was covered with white plaster like the floor. A puzzling place is at AY, a corner of a house. The ground is about 750 level; on entering a narrow doorway, a step up is at 792; on ascending, a 1-in. plastered floor at 781 is seen with a slightly lower portion on the right. Being so much raised, it cannot be a bath; is it possibly a kind of shrine?

29. In DR there are two square pits sunk in the native sandstone. Around the southern one is a walling of brick. The sandstone here is at 583 level, forming the floor of the room. In DR a cattle trough was built at a higher level, in a re-use of the room. Similarly, in later uses of rooms AS and C, cattle troughs were added. When the city was declining, the disused buildings were evidently used for stables, just as is the case at present in Gaza.

The Greek letters on various parts show to what group of brick sizes the walls belong. The varieties of bricks are shown in diagram, pl. li, with the letters which serve to distinguish them. The practical use of the letters is to indicate what walls belong to a contemporary group of building (see sect. 48).

CHAPTER IV

OBJECTS OF THE CANAANITE PERIOD

30. FROM the preceding details of the city, it is clear that the Canaanite was at the same standard,

in the general comfort of life, as the Judaeo-Greek population of two thousand years later. The layout of the buildings is quite equal to that of the Seleucidan Sandehanna.

The small objects which are of the same age should now be noted. Nearly two hundred scarabs were found, and these are of the greatest value for dating the deposits. They are here grouped according to the position of finding. The upper level of the city is marked as level II, the top dust being level I. The chamber in which each was found is stated by the letters below on the right.

31. Pl. XIII. The seven small scarabs, 2–8, found in Q are useful as dating those types to Apepa I. 21 is a cylinder with cross lines. 23 is of a Treasurer Senba, who also appears on a stele at Leyden, of a Fayum family (*Lieb.*, 371), and on a Vienna stele, 69 (*Lieb.*, 353). The delicately cut scarab, 26, in a thin gold frame, is of the great scribe of the Treasurer Nehes-kap, " a negro of the king's household," a man already known on a coarse scarab (*Scarabs*, xvii, BD). The type of the haematite cylinder, 33, is well known (see Hayes Ward, 83–88, 95, 99, 899, but this most resembles 900, of Syro-Hittite work, though none of these are as well engraved as no. 26; 900 is from Kul-tepe in Cappadocia). 35, with two men and daggers, recurs in 54.

Level II. 43 is a carnelian bead with the name Amenemhat finely engraved, but proved by the reversed A to be of Canaanite workmanship.

It was with the silver crescent in a grain pit, AT, on the edge of the wady, levelled 760–659. The others here were picked up during the work, 44 of Apepa I, 45 of Ysaanen or Ysaan of the sea, a new Hyksos name.

32. Level III. This is the level under the burnt layer, probably of xiith dyn. 67 reads " maker of *rb* Ptah-mery." *Rb*, or *lb*, is supposed to be the name of a vase; but as the vase here is represented as tied up, it more likely refers to the contents, possibly an abbreviation of *laboneh*, incense. The types 68–72, 77, all occur in the xiith dyn. (see *Illahun*, ix, x). The other modified Egyptian types, which are usually called Hyksos, are more probably of Canaanite work, especially as we have no proof that the Hyksos were already in touch with Egyptian style during the xiith dyn.

33. Pl. XIV. The scarabs from the cemeteries have the tomb number at bottom right hand. No. 93 is of Sma-ka-ra, of whom two scarabs of quite a different style are known (sc. xx, Q, R). The 291

group is only from a common burial ground, and not of a single period. 113 reads *yaz sna' mera* " May Yaz comfort Mera "; *sna'*, comfort, literally " make smooth," applies both to mind and body, as in the royal name *Ra-sna'-ab*: " May Ra comfort the heart." The name Yaz probably refers to a Tyrian god, as Yazebaal (Jezebel), or " Yaz is lord," came from Tyre.

Nos. 126–40 all come from late cemeteries, not from the early groups. Site 291 is a remarkable mass of human and animal bones crushed together, about 15 in. deep and 5 or 6 ft. wide. As there was no respect or order shown, and six gold hair-rings (xv, 3) and many scarabs were included, it was probably a plague pit.   xviiith dyn.

141–2 are from a cemetery of the xviiith dyn. in the valley, tomb 801.

Unknown positions. These were brought up by workers as casually found : 143 of Apepa I; 144 from a grave about 110–119 of Oa " the great," one of the sea kings, *mu*, of the xvith dyn.

171–2 are seals of red and white limestone, probably foreign.

189 Rahetep, was bought, not from Ajjūl. It is the best out of all the examples of this king.

197 is a domed seal of haematite, with a rude figure of a quadruped.

34. JEWELLERY. XV, 1. Silver crescent pendant, found with carnelian bead inscribed Amenemhat. From the fine work, probably Amenemhat I; but as this is Palestine work (by the reversed A), it may not keep step with Egypt.

xv, 2. Gold pendant, embossed, and covered with granules; in form of a falcon with wings curved upward. Only eight examples of granulated work are known as early. Weight 125·4 grs., Babylonian unit (Jerusalem). Found in roadway, pl. iv. This had evidently been dropped by a lady, and lost in the mud. It lay there perfectly bright and unaltered, till in lowering the road our workmen found it in a lump of earth, and of course brought it up.

xv, 3. Gold hair-rings, of usual form (*Objects of Daily Use*, xvii). These were all in a mass of crushed bones, human and animal, with scarabs of early xviiith dyn. (see above, sect. 33). The weights are, 117, 63·3, and 62·4 grs., Babylonian. With these was a dump of rough gold.

xv, 4. Gold toggle-pin 78·3 grs., ear-rings 77·9 grs., scarabs (see 113 above), and string of carnelian beads. From grave 2 in the city (Jerusalem Mus.). The gold is of the Syrian necef unit.

xv, 5. Half of a bar of quartz carved with a lion head at the end. The other half is exactly similar. It was found in one of the port-holes of the tunnel. The purpose is unknown ; possibly a girdle fastener (Jerusalem and London).

xv, 6. Two gold ear-rings (85·5 grs.), with gold and stone beads on the bar. Carnelian beads, and scarab 89. From tomb 187 (New York).

An electrum toggle-pin, with plain square shank, was in the town (London).

A plain band of silver was across the forehead of a child in grave I in the city. With scarab 112 and pottery (Jerusalem).

35. BRONZE. From Rooms in city. xvi, 1, Thin dagger with wide end (broken) from AC. 2, Curved knife, of Hyksos period. 3, Thick dagger, N, level 761. 4, Thick dagger, AW. 5, Thin dagger, D 784, rivet holes. 6, 7, Toggle-pins. 8 (New York), 9, Tweezers. 10–15, Needles. 16, Spear butt. 17, Unknown tool. 18, Wide lance head. 20, Link. 21, Bracelet (?). 22, Double hook. 23, Adze with binding (New York). IRON. 24, Knife, top. 25, Large knife, AG. 26, Nail top.

36. XVII. xiith dyn. Low city. 27, 28, Copper rods. 29, Needle. 35, 36, Rods. 30, Thin dagger (Jerusalem). 31, 32, Daggers. 33, Dagger with rivets for handle. 34, Hyksos curved knife (see sect. 8). 38–9, Lance heads. 40, Whetstone.

XVIII (see 47, 46, 30, 2, 41, 42). Bronze knife, grave 804, xviiith dyn. 43, Chisel. Small objects, (see sect. 3).

XIX. Tombs, Hyksos Age. 41, Half-socketed dagger (see Beth-pelet, xi, 82). 42, Thin dagger. 43, Chisels (41–3, Jerusalem). 44–5, Toggle-pins. 46–9, see Copper Age, sect. 56.

XX. Upper City. 50–61, Lance heads. 69, Small thin dagger. 71, Block of bronze. 72, Similar block of pottery, of unknown use. 73, Bronze rod. 74–80, Toggle-pins. 81. A spiked cylinder, too small for a weapon, possibly a spiked wheel of a model chariot. 83, Chisel. 84, Adze, found in a pit full of rubbish in the plain (Jerusalem). 85, 86, Rymers. 70, Needle.

XXI. Hyksos Tombs. 88–96, Bronze toggle-pins. 97–8, Others of bone. 100–105, Lance heads. 98, 104, Of unknown use.

37. 99, 107, Seated figure of Hor-ka (pl. xxii). This is of hard grey limestone, 7·8 ins. high, base 6·3×3·8. The face and front edge are bruised and worn. The right eye has the eyebrow ridge and outer corner cut sharply, the other eye not so worked.

The hands, in the usual position on the knees, are poorly done. The heavy ridge coming forward from the ankle bone is un-Egyptian. The whole work is a good imitation, but not truly Egyptian. The same is true of the inscription, where Ptah-seker is written serek, transposing two signs. It reads, " The devoted to Ptah-seker, Intendant of the guard of the interior, Hor-ka." The interior may refer to a province or to the palace. Along the front edge are traces of signs more than half worn away, and not intelligible.

38. 114, Amulets. 112, Leaden figure of Hathor, found with lance heads, 257, and 109, ear-ring (?). 108, Ring, grave 13. 110, Needle, tomb 257. 116. Bronze wig curler, xviiith dyn. 117, Razor, group 291, xviiith dyn. 118, Egyptian axe, found alone in pit, xviiith dyn.

39. XXII, XXIII. BONE applied. The pattern of the box, as found and as restored, is given in xxii (Jerusalem). It is drawn in xxiii, 5. Also a smaller box 263 (London). Another box with birds, as the large one, is in New York. Such applied work with bird figures was found in the Hyksos deposit (see Sedment, xl, xli, at Univ. Coll.). XXIII, 1, Segment of ivory, for gaming (?). 2, Mother of pearl ring. 3, Ivory stud. (1–3 xiith dyn.) 4, Bodkin. 6, Beads. 7, 9, Needles. 8, Pin. 10, Uraeus on pin. 11, Die, of pyramidal form known in Palestine. 12, 15, 16, Slips for decoration. 13, Buttons (?). 14, Disc for attachment. 17, Slips from a box. 18–24, Slips for decoration. 25, from top of Tell.

40. XXIV, XXV. Alabaster vases. These are usually of Egyptian alabaster, but many are of Syrian work. XXV, 1, may be the base of a tazza. 2 seems to be the bottom of a large pilgrim bottle, carved as if cased with rush or string ; the stone is black and white porphyry. 3 is the base of a large trachyte vase, of xiith dyn. 4, A rude bowl of basalt. 5, A typical xiith-dyn. vase from Egypt. 6, A rude bowl, Syrian. 7, 8, Tazzas of gypsum of Egyptian xviiith-dyn. shape ; from Beth-pelet. These are proved to be Syrian work by two arcs of circles struck on the base of one, in a tentative marking of the block ; no Egyptian used compasses. 9, 10, 11 are imitated from Cretan types. 9 was with 39, which is Syrian. 12 to 20 would be possibly Egyptian, but the flatted base of some looks more like Syrian work. 21 seems to echo the Copper Age forms of pl. xli. 22 is incomplete, a neck-piece has been ground to fit it. 23, 24, 27, 28 may be

Egyptian, but 25, 26 are Syrian. 31, 32, 33, 35, 36, 37 are kohl pots which are probably Egyptian, as the Syrian used a tube or horn, which was later adopted in Egypt under Tehutmes III. 38, 39 are certainly Syrian, by the work and form of handle.

On XXIV the large maul is of hard limestone; next to it the hafted pick is of basalt; both are from the Hyksos level of the city. At the base of the plate is a rude head of pottery, an elementary head of limestone, and a horse's head and neck of brown pottery showing the kind of mane of the Hyksos horses. The little dove pendant is in xxi, 14. Below is a bossy bead of silver. At the end is a pottery wheel of a model waggon of xiith dyn. (see pl. l, 99).

CHAPTER V

POTTERY

41. XXVI, XXVII. SELECTED examples of pottery. Nos. 1, 2, 3, 5, 13, 16 are of the Copper Age. In the Bronze Age the earlier stage is marked by the shoulder handle, as 4, 6, 7, 10, 23; the handle joining to the top of the neck is later. The knob on the handle in 10, 23 is for the thumb to prevent it slipping when tilted over. The forms of this period are the best. In the next stage the forms are clumsy, as 24, 25, 40. In the later Bronze Age of the xviiith dyn. the Egyptian jar 12, without handle, appears. The earlier forms are suave and unified, as in 6; later there is a fashion of abrupt lines and breaks in the curves, as in 18 or 26. The thin brown pottery of Cyprus or North Syria, 35–38, is an imitation of leather work, which was largely imported into Egypt under Tehutmes III. The ox-form bottle is Cypriote. The incised patterns, 45, have usually been credited to the Early Bronze Age; but they are found here all through the time from Apepa back to the xiith dyn. On pl. xxxvi it appears that the origin is from a wreath pattern, 1, 2, 3, coarsely copied.

42. XXXVII–L. The additions to the Corpus of Pottery follow the system already adopted. The general type number is at the left side of the page, the subtype letter and variety number are at the right top of each drawing. The place reference is at the right base of the drawing.

This notation follows that on the site plans, LIV, LV, *Top* refers to the loose earth of about 2 ft. above the walls. II is the Hyksos level of the xvth dyn.; separate chambers have a single letter, or

have A or B prefixed to that. III, or with C or D prefixed, is the xiith dyn. level (beneath the burnt stratum), which is planned with outlines on pl. liv. The references of CD often have the level in inches added, from 583 up to about 730. The actual burnt stratum is between 726 and 744 level. The simple numbers between 1 and 500, and of 800 upwards, are tomb numbers, as on LV plan, and LIX to LXI registers. For instance, in XL, type 28 N 3 is found in tomb 163, in chamber AQ of Hyksos age, and in chamber DF at 675 level.

On Register LIX are stated the Copper Age types, which are very few. There are only the flat-based bowl with bands, 6 R; the tiny cup, 10 Z; the flat bowl without bands, 22 N 6; the flat bowl with slight bulge, 24 F; the cylindrical cup, 29 Z; the great ovate jars, 30 G, some with a spout, 30 J; the wide-necked jar, 33 M, with handles; rarely without, 30 H; and the similar bottles, 69 L; these are the total of this age, while not one of these appears later. There was an entire break in the history of form, and also of fabric, as the material is all soft buff or drab paste, lightly baked. This age was parallel with the pyramid period of vth and vith dyns. in Egypt.

Of the age of the xiith and xvth dyns., the types found in the city are listed on lxii in parallel lines, so as to show how far the types were continuous. Only about a tenth of the varieties continued alike in both stages. This may be due to the Hyksos movement arresting part of the Canaanite civilisation, while pushing in fresh elements from the north.

The whole system of pottery registration will have, of course, to be recast in the future, when the varieties are all known and dated. In the present age of growth of study, all that can be done is to have a storage system for keeping the material accessible and comparable, until there is no prospect of further additions. In this year's work the Copper Age types are all new to us, as well as many later varieties.

43. The painted pottery, pls. xxviii–xxxv, is numbered continuously for convenience of reference. As being distinctively different from the known products of Palestine (where we only meet with crude daubs in red, like 104), the connection with other lands is of much historic meaning. Only two or three scraps, of the quality here found, are recorded from other sites. The reason may be that very few of the towns before 2000 B.C. have yet been widely cleared: moreover, Gaza was the most important trading city, and had almost the only good port. None of this pottery is known in Egypt, which

2

points to its rise being in the poor age of the xiiith-xviith dyns., when trade was restrained.

It is evident that all from 1–20 belong to one group, and probably others on to 33. A rather coarser cross-hatching goes from 37–51, which is probably of the same region; compare the fish on 5 and 51. Among these is obviously one piece of Palestinian style, 43. Where does this grand class originate? The pottery itself is boldly formed, of fine hard paste, with perfectly smooth face. The weaving plait pattern is almost peculiar to the Mediterranean: it is found in Egypt, Crete, Rhodes, Italy, Spain, and Britain (*Dec. Pat.*, lxvi), rarely in Sumeria, crudely in Susa, but it does not appear in Cappadocia. The union-jack square, 5, 27, 28, occurs in Cyprus (*D.P.* YM 9); but the shaded diagonal, 30, is both Asiatic and Western (*D.P.* YO, Q). The disc cut into eighths is in Egypt, Cilicia, Crete, and Italy (*D.P.* OB, C). The Maltese Cross, 23–26, is archaic at Susa, and is in Crete and Italy (*D.P.* SA to L). Therefore, all these are Mediterranean designs, but some may be Asiatic. The latitude is limited by the palm tree, 6, which extended to Cilicia and Assyria, but precludes North Syria or Cappadocia. Altogether Cilicia seems to be the most likely source for this work, and this is in accord with the high state of civilisation of the Keftiu soon after this period.

No. 4 fragment has lost the head of the bird, but a head of the same style was found, probably from the same jar, and is here added. No. 5 is the largest, and nearly all the figures remain; possibly the rest may yet be found in the pit. It is very peculiar in having two figures of birds, faintly traced in red, on the backs of the other figures. The inner line of the body is marked with black dots. These birds fit too closely to their position to have been outlines for a disused design.

44. XXXI. Nos. 41, 42, from a bull figure, probably belong together. The bird figures, 44–46, are spirited, and belong to the preceding style. The cross-lined style 47–51 is coarser.

No. 54 is a crude notched pattern on a raised cross and circle, apparently the top of a heavy, coarse lid for a jar. Of xiith dyn.

Nos. 55–62 are of a remarkable class of ware; the surface creamy white and glossy, the body quite white, the colouring chocolate, with burnt sienna bordering in 62. It is the finest ancient fabric known. The source is Mediterranean, by the spiral 59. The chequers, 56, is Cappadocian and South

Anatolian. The nearest comparison is that from Gordion, but the colouring is not quite the same.

The coarse patterns 63–77 are probably local imitations of the finer wares. The large jar, 78, of which the outline is below, looks more like the regulated style of Hittite work.

45. XXXIV is of Cypriote ware of the usual forked-handle type (see xxxviii, 19). Here also are pieces of the same pattern, but much finer in painting and thinner in body, painted with red, as well as black, with detail not known on Cypriote ware, as 85–90. These seem to belong to a class of Anatolian (? Cilician) work, which was copied in Cyprus. The limit between the original and the copy is not yet defined. Many pieces of the black ware with red lines parallel were found, 102, 103, and this extends back to the xiith dyn. The lines were evidently put on with a row of brushes fixed together. A large vase of the same kind was found at Beth-pelet (see *Corpus*, 68, R 2).

46. XXXV. A few pieces of Palestinian decoration were found, 104–108. 106, 107 are different vases, but serve to explain each other. These are far inferior to the later examples of the xixth dyn. from Beth-pelet. 112, 113 are examples of the serpent ascending the handle of a vase. 114 is a bird-spout. 115, 116 are of different bowls, but serve to explain the pattern; this form of lotus is probably of the Assyrian period; both pieces were found on the surface. On the surface also were scraps of Philistine ware, 118, and of the red polished flasks of xviiith dyn., thus agreeing with the ruins being earlier than that date. The Arab painted pot, 120, was also on the top.

For pls. xxxvi–l, see after xxvii described before.

47. LI. Many weights were found in the city, nearly all in the upper level, of the Hyksos age. The interest lies in the evidence of trade. The Egyptian qedet is the largest class, as might be expected on the frontier. The necef of Syria is common, but the khoirine is very scarce. The beqa may be from any source, as it was the Egyptian gold weight, and is also found in Sumeria and at Mohenjo-daro.

48. The sizes of bricks are a valuable clue to the connection of different buildings in a town. Many bricks were measured, and are dealt with here as in the volume *Beth-pelet* I. A diagram is formed of the length and width (in inches along the sides), and, on marking in the results, it is seen how certain groups can be distinguished. The numbers refer to the

places, but it seems too confusing to add them to the plan. What is best is to use a Greek letter for each distinct group, and then to place that letter on each wall that was noted. The letters are the same as at Beth-pelet. Where fresh types occur they are marked with Hebrew letters nearest related to the Greek. This method enables a reader quickly to see on the plan which walls are likely to be contemporary.

49. LII. Plan of a kiln of which the table has disappeared, but the tall bricks which supported it are still in place : they are 20–22 ins. long, 14–17 wide, and 4–5·4 thick. The wind hole was at the west end, and the spring of an arch at each side showed where the furnace began. On the north side are holes at 28 ins. over the floor, i.e. at the level of the table of 6 ins. thick upon the bricks. These flue holes run back to the sides of the hole in which the furnace was built. The view from the south-east corner is at the base of pl. vi. These bricks are the usual *sigma* size used in building (see sect. 26).

50. Nos. 2–7 are various club mace-heads of stone, mostly of the xiith dyn. 9 is a curious block which seems to be part of a mould. 10 is one of three potter's turn-tables : the block was set in the ground, and a disc of wood, with a peg to go in the hole, was turned round on it by hand : in Neolithic times the right hand did the turning and the left modelled the clay. 11–13, Spindle whorls. 14, Plummet (?). 15, Pendant. 16, A gaming piece. 19, 20, Heads of walking-staves. 21–3, stands for grinding food.

LIII. For the Tell, see sects. 5–8.

LIV. For the city plan, see sects. 9–12, 22–9.

CHAPTER VI

THE COPPER AGE

51. IN the general account of the Tell, sect. 8, the principal work of the Copper Age has been noticed, the Great Fosse around three sides of the hill. A view of this is given in xii, 1, showing a stripe of the long smooth *glacis* exposed in the trench. Incidentally this is of great interest, as illustrating modern Bedawy mentality. The diggers were told to leave ledges at the side at a man's height apart, for safety ; without any other direction, two new men, quite untrained, cut the sides as regularly as masonry. This shows what unexpected capacities these people have latent.

The Great Fosse must have been nearly 4,000 ft. long, 35 ft. wide, and averaging 12 ft. deep, a removal of some 250,000 tons of soil. The full detail of shape cannot be recovered, as it extends below the present water-table. The main gate into the city was at a bridge left across the fosse at the north-east side. This causeway has not yet been uncovered in detail, but in pl. lviii, at the top left, is marked the north side of the causeway. It was certainly 25 ft. wide or more. Below is marked the outer side of the Great Fosse, and its turn to the south side of the causeway. All this is buried under 15 or 20 ft. of washed-down soil, which we hope to remove further.

52. LVIII. From the causeway line there ran a tunnel for 500 ft. outward into the open plain. The floor of the tunnel is about on the top of the sandstone of the causeway. There must therefore have been a large mass of soil, at a higher level than the sandstone causeway, in which the tunnel was excavated. The whole plan is obscured by denudation, which has removed the tunnel entirely at the inner end, where it disappears, worn away by a water channel cut by denudation in the sandstone. The ground here is covered with a dense brown clay in which we have cleared out the line of the tunnel. From a complete passage only a hundred feet away, it gradually shades off until the last trace ends at the gateway. At I the tunnel is complete, but the roof fallen ; at II only 52 ins. of height was left, filled in with rain-laid clay ; at III is a false opening ; at IV only 42 ins. left ; at V only 2 ins. left, cut off by a water-course. Much more clearance and complete levelling is needed to explain the changes at the entrance, but we can at least see that the tunnel must belong to the early works of the Copper Age, as it preceded the denudation period.

53. LVIII. The plan of the tunnel is divided in halves here, the outer half placed below, the division at A, A. The inner end of it has fallen in at many parts (see xii, 3), obscuring what were the original openings for removing the material. The outer end has three portholes remaining complete, see xii, 4. These open in the upper half of the tunnel, with a flat bottom on which the blocking material could rest. The height of the tunnel varies from 73 to 53 ins., as marked here. The width varies between 33 and 53 ins. Evidently the cutting was begun from the outer end, for at the most southerly part the cut ran too far, and was backed a little. The cause of the bend southward is not known ;

there were no tombs in the way. At the part where the height is marked 53 there is a groove up each side of the tunnel. This is 11 ins. wide on west, 9 on east, and it rises 8 and 21 ins. respectively into the roof. Evidently these grooves were to hold posts firmly at the sides for a door, or for a barring of the way. There are also similar traces of a doorway nearer to the outer end. These suggest that the tunnel was for access, and was to be closed to intruders. In the tunnel were burials, upon partial filling, of the xvith and xviiith dyns. ; these prove that the tunnel was disused before then, and probably before the Hyksos Age. At the outer end the tunnel opens into a pit (see xii, 2).

54. LV. The plan of the cemetery has the earlier tombs marked solid black. They are proved by their pottery to belong to the Copper Age. Some other tombs without pottery may belong to the same age. It is evident that the tombs and tunnel are so placed to avoid contact. Possibly the tunnel was being pushed from the inner end, until it was realised that the tombs were in the way, and then the work from the other end was carried around the tombs to meet the finished part. Or the tunnel may have been swerved for some other reason, and the tombs extended up to it.

55. At the outer end of the tunnel a sunk road runs southward, though the steps out of the tunnel do not lead into it. This sunk road, cut in the sandstone, seems too wide to have been formerly roofed over as a tunnel (see ii, 5). It does not run on, north of the tunnel, so it is presumably a later work, the tunnel steps being independent. It is linked up to two large pits, which again are linked with a wide sunk road running eastward (see ii. 4, looking west). The eastern end has not been uncovered yet. It seems likely to run into a vast fosse 25 ft. wide and almost as deep ; this has not

yet been cleared to the bottom, nor the extent of it ascertained. All these works out in the open field are unintelligible until the extent, connections, and levels can be traced. The tunnel seems intended to lead upward, at the end of the fosse. At the south end of our working are other deep cuttings which cannot yet be explained.

56. Very few weapons remained of the Copper Age. The most important is the fine rapier, 17 ins. long (xviii, 1 ; xix, 47) ; the mid rib and slightly hollowed faces suggest Cyprus as the source. The dagger with skew handle, (xviii 2 ; xix, 46) is from an undated tomb, but the smooth face and metallic state show it to be copper. The handle was of bone, but so decayed that the form could only be preserved with paraffin wax. Anomalous narrow daggers (xix, 48, 49) are of copper with smooth surface, and 49 is dated by Copper Age pottery. Such a form is, so far, unknown ; it had a short handle, proved by the turn-over of the tang, so these were daggers and not lances.

The pottery of this age is specified in sects. 41, 42. It is different both in form and quality from any of the Canaanite period. The whole of the Copper Age civilisation was entirely wiped out by the invasion of the North Syrian button-badge people, on their way to the conquest of Egypt. Nothing of pottery, weapons, or type of tombs survived ; entirely new traditions came in at the age of the xiith dyn., with people who were probably the Canaanites of literary record.

LIX. Register of tombs of the Copper Age, as proved by the pottery.

LX, LXI. Register of tombs of the Hyksos Age.

LXII. Types of pottery which can be distinguished as of xiith and xvth dyns. by their position in the city levels.

The places to which objects have been assigned are marked by initial letters on the plates at the top left side. A Aberdeen. B Bolton. Bd Bedford. C Cambridge Ethnol. F Fitzwilliam, Cambridge. H Hampstead. J Jerusalem. L London. M Manchester. N Newcastle. NY New York. R Rochdale. T Tokyo.

INDEX

GAZA. 1. TWO BODIES AND HORSE. 2, 3, 4. HORSE IN PIT AND BURIALS. 5, 6. ASSES AND BURIAL, 101.

VIII

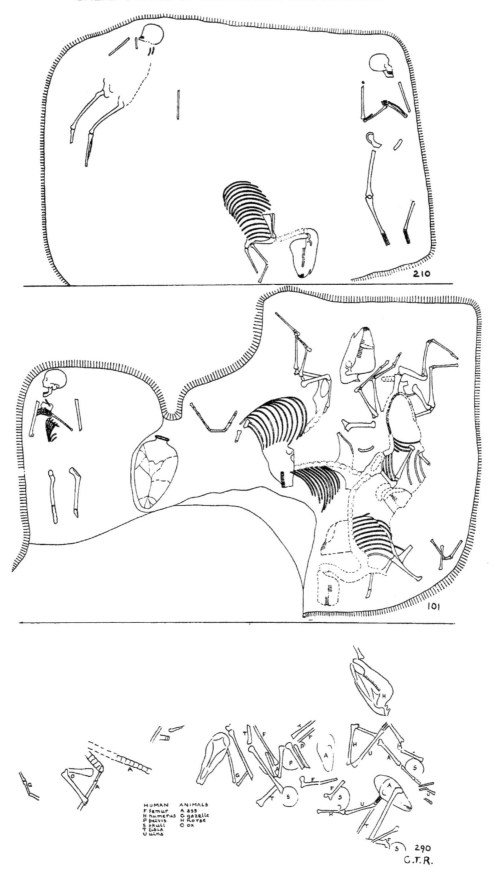

HUMAN
F femur
H humerus
P pelvis
S skull
T tibia
U ulna

ANIMALS
A ass
G gazelle
H horse
O ox

210

101

290

C.T.R.

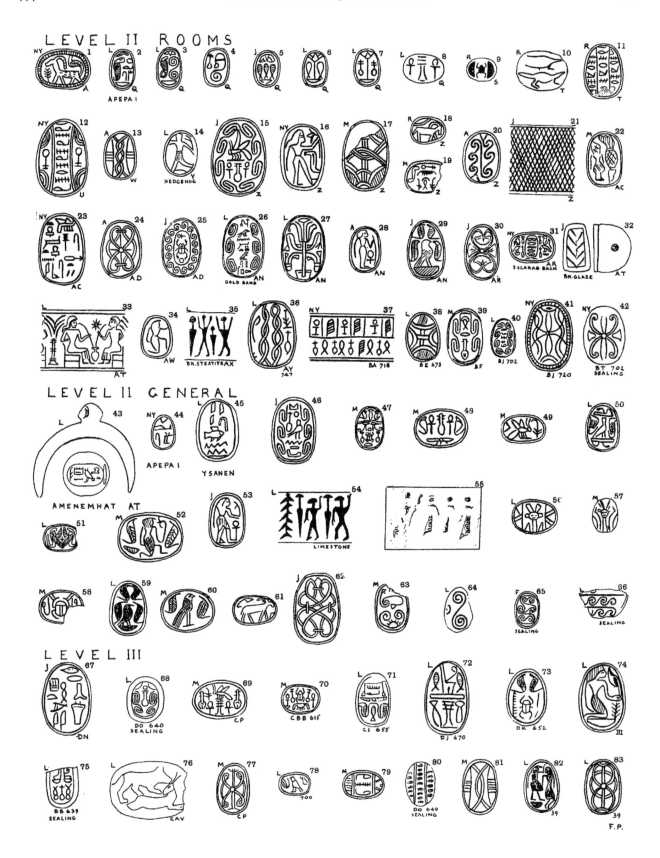

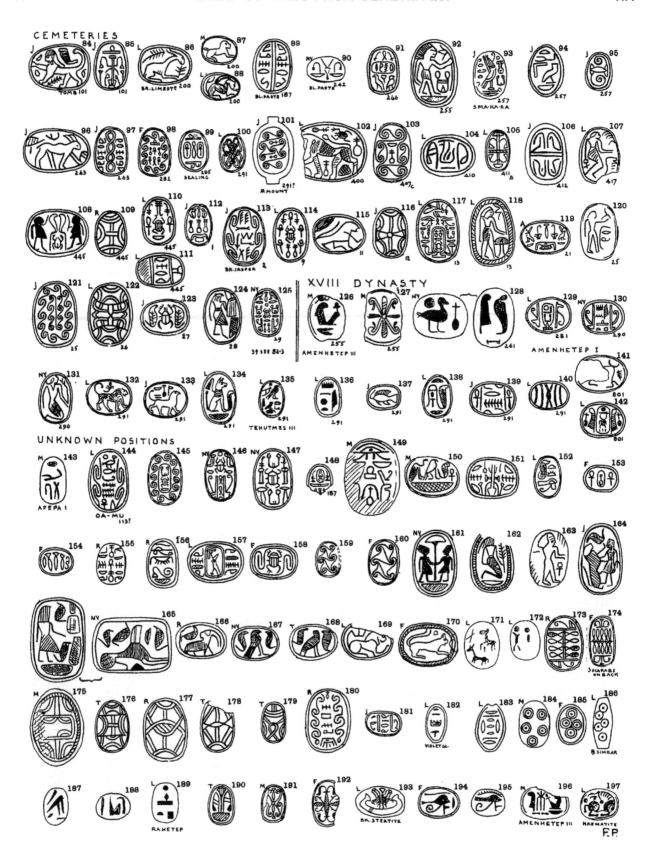

CEMETERIES

XVIII DYNASTY

UNKNOWN POSITIONS

F.P.

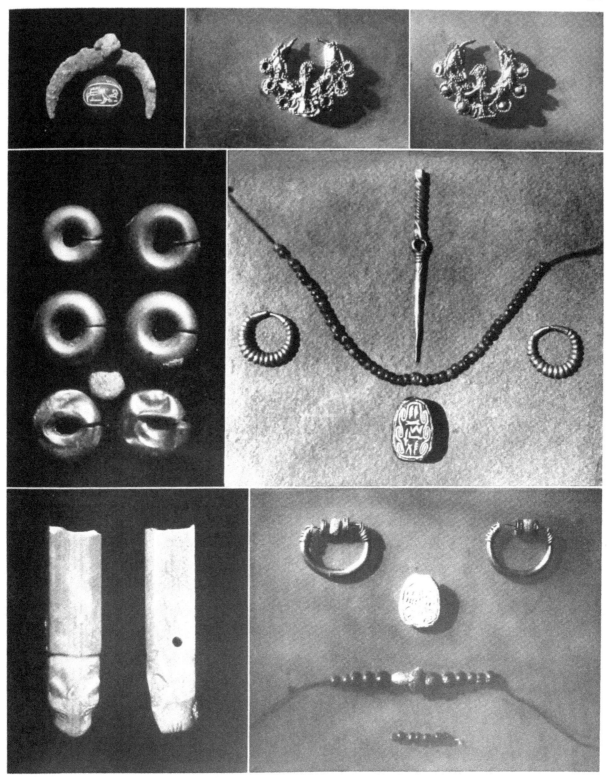

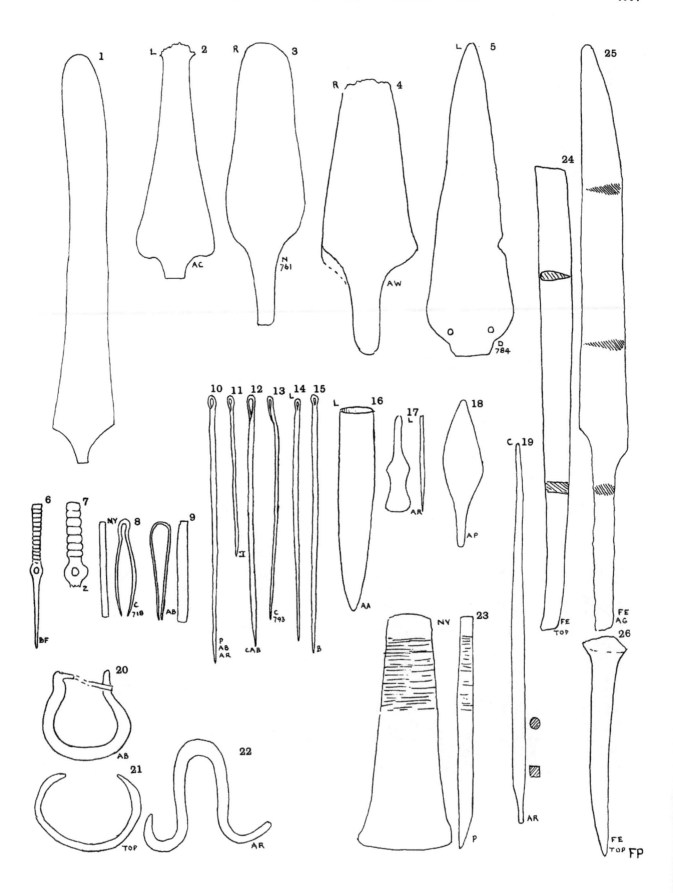

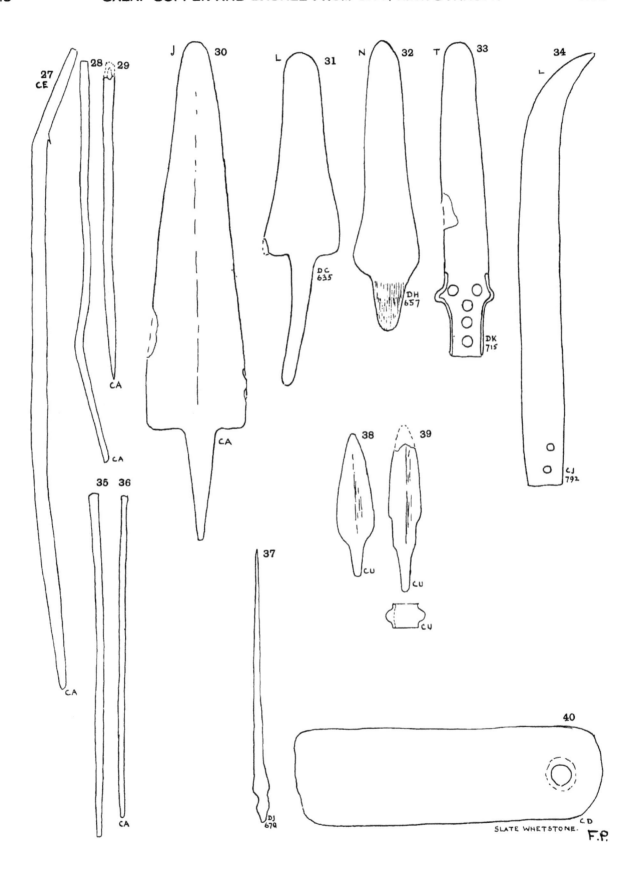

SLATE WHETSTONE.

F.P.

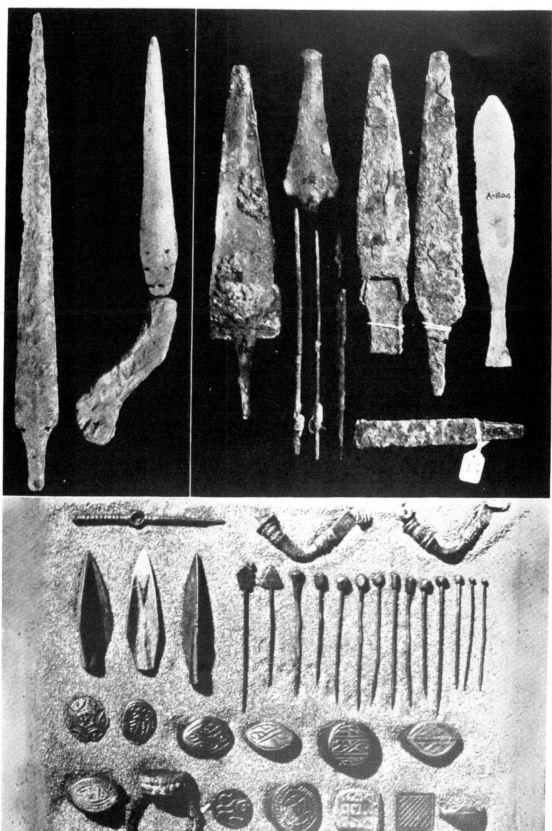

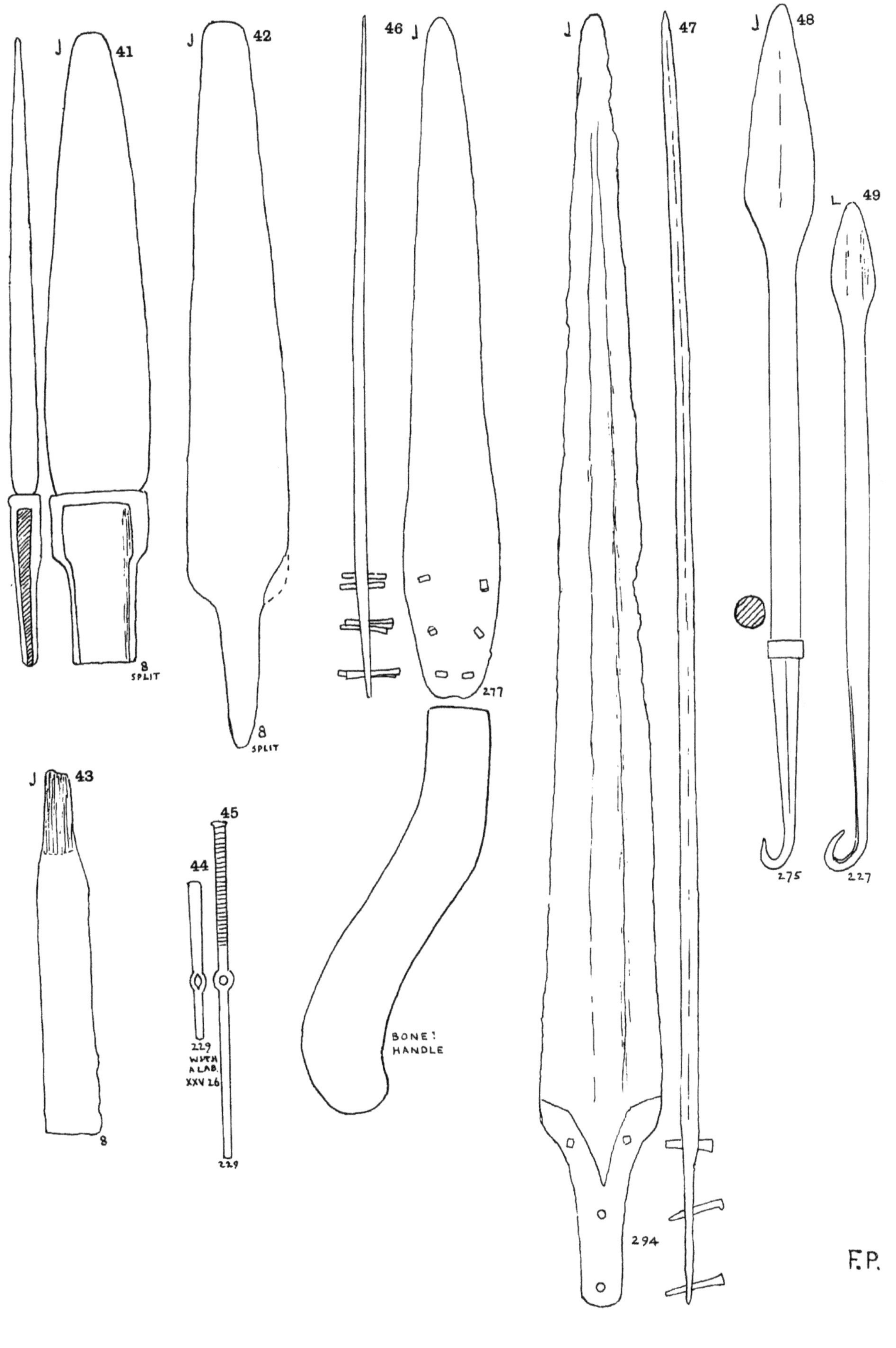

J 41

J 42

46 J

J

47

J 48

L 49

8 SPLIT

8 SPLIT

277

J 43

45

44

229
WITH
A LAB.
XXV 26

229

8

BONE
HANDLE

294

275

227

F.P.

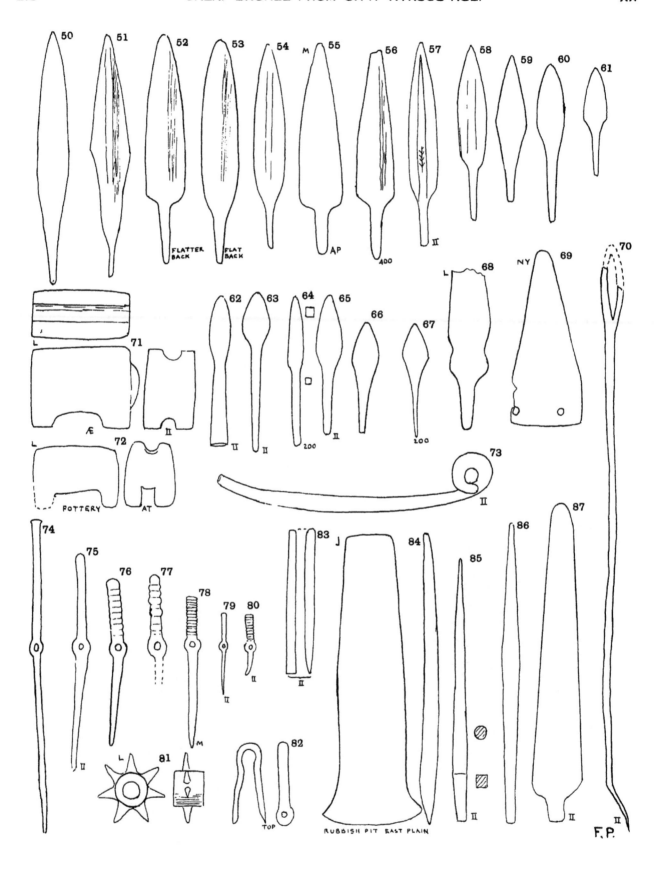

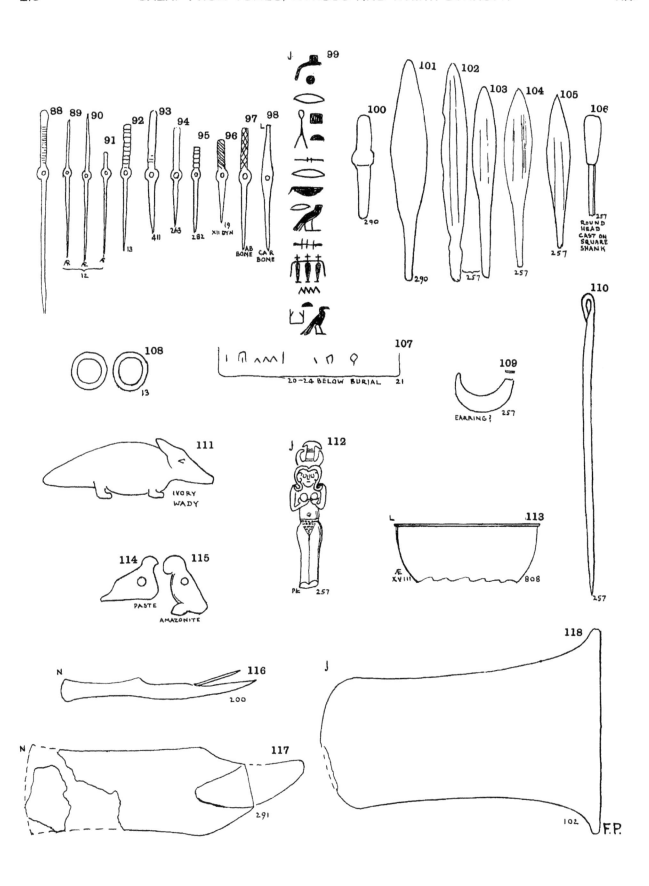

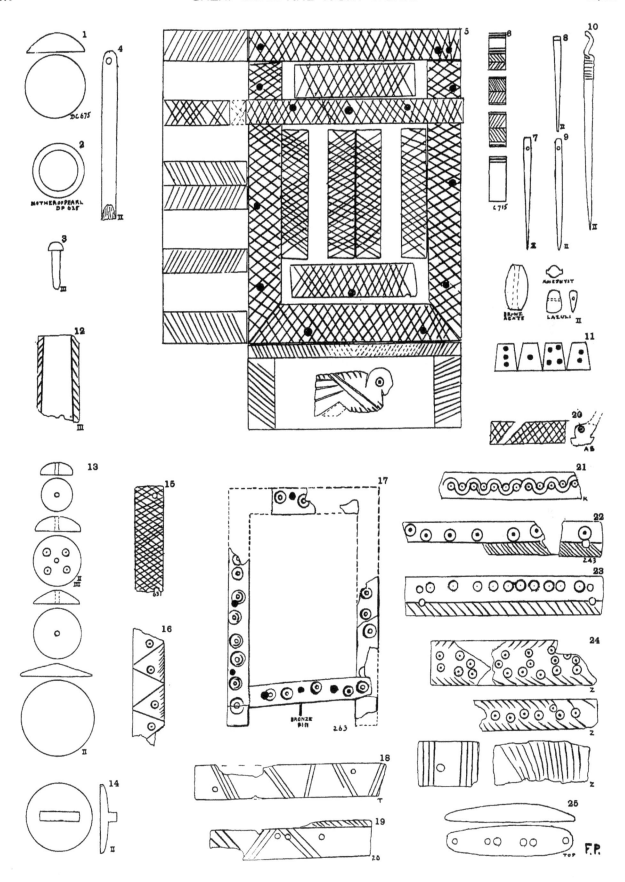

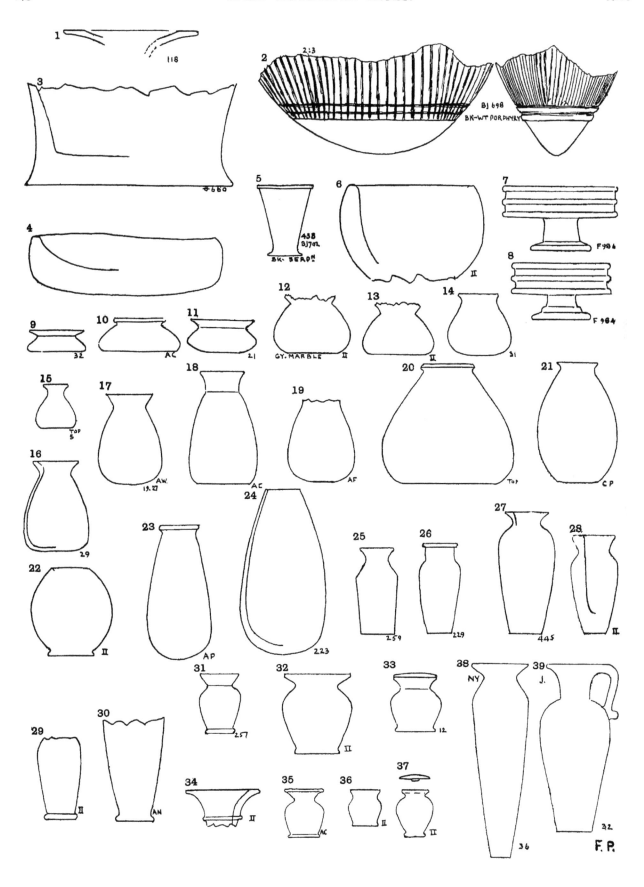

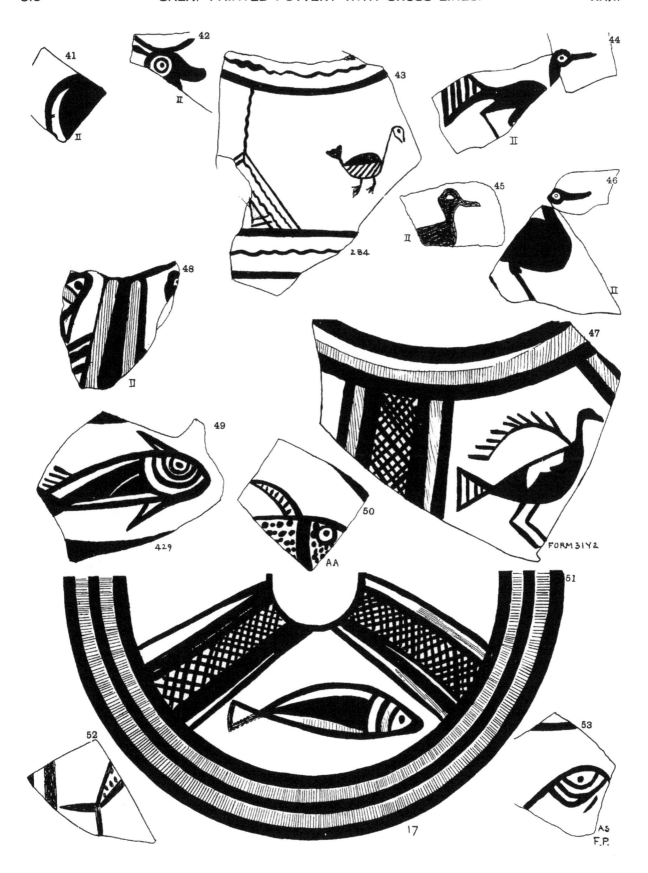

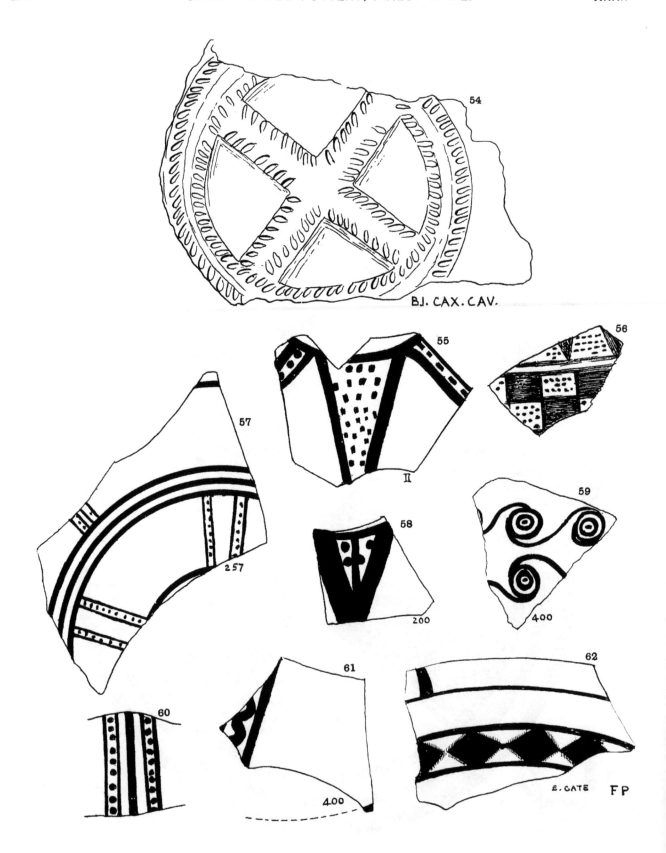

BJ. CAX. CAV.

E. CATE   FP

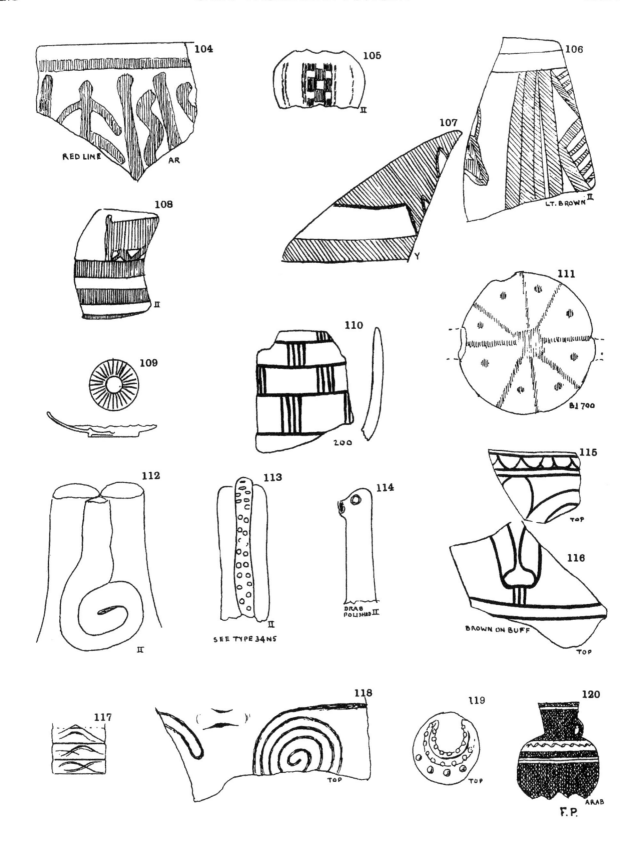

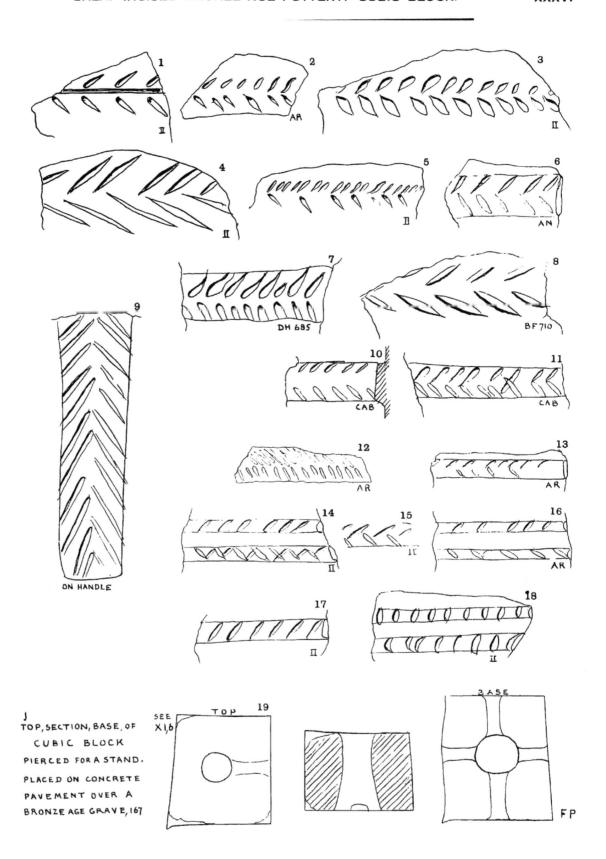

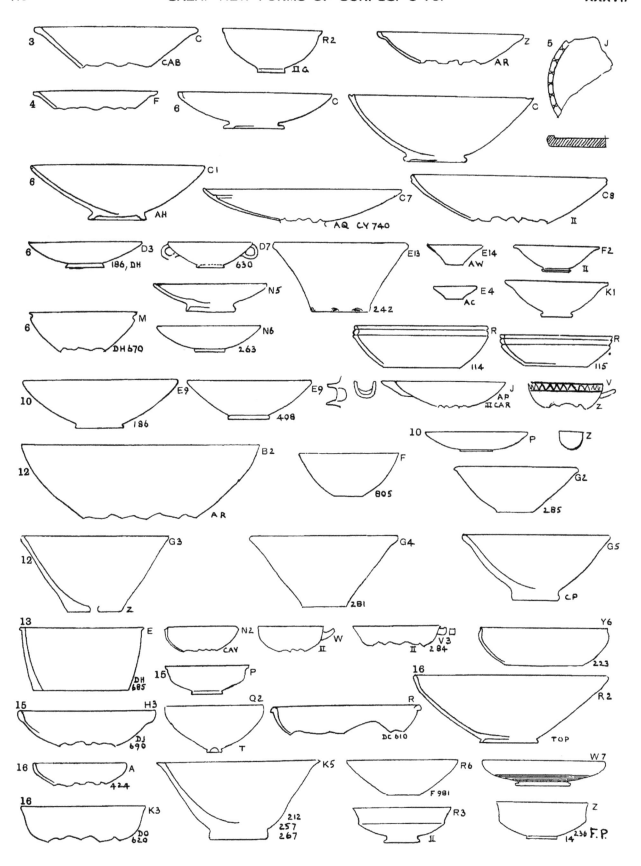

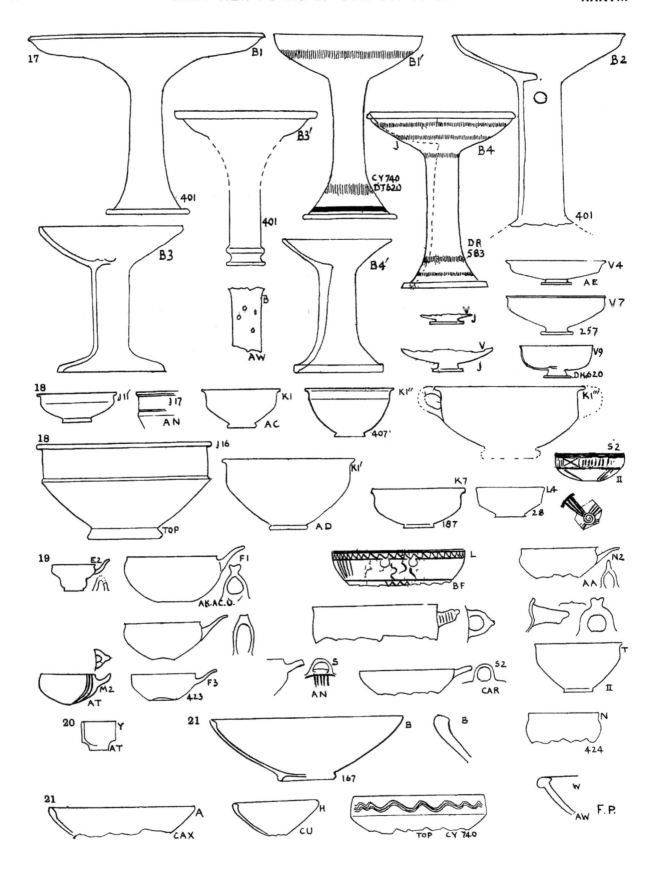

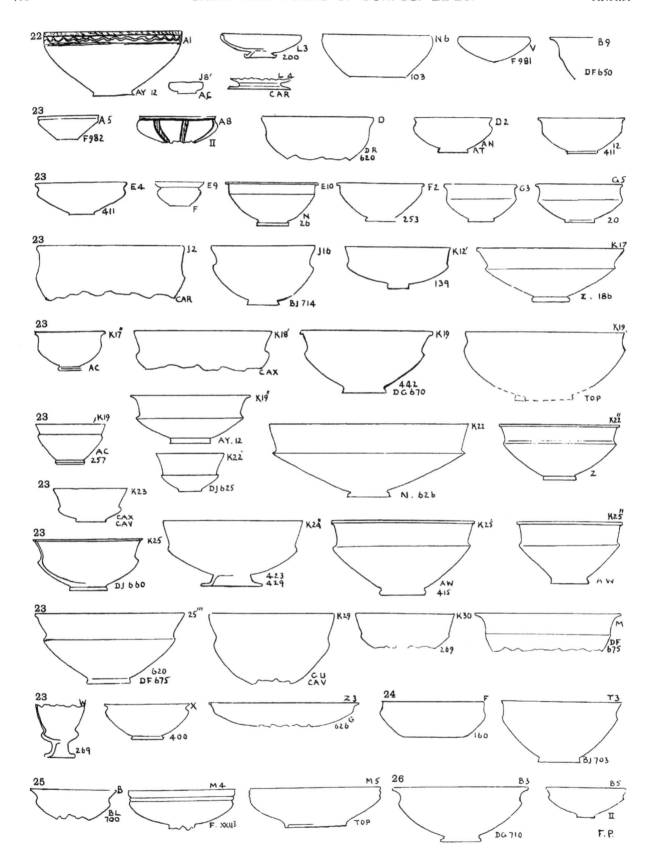

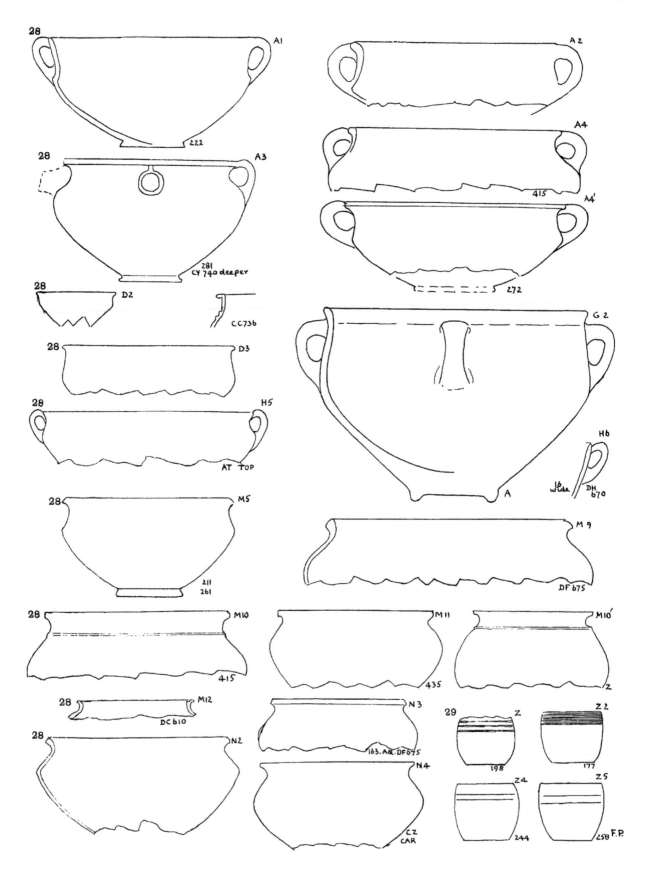

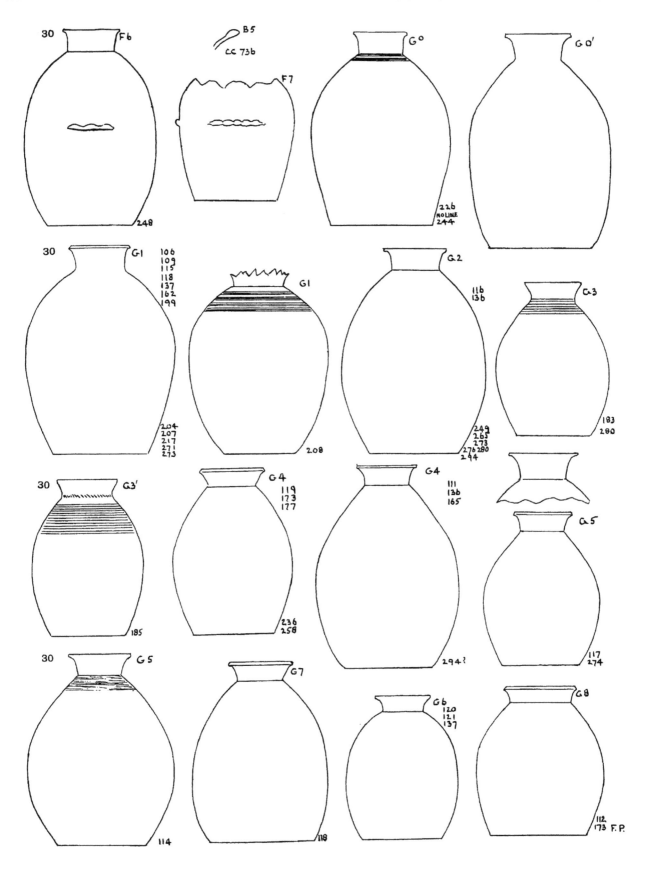

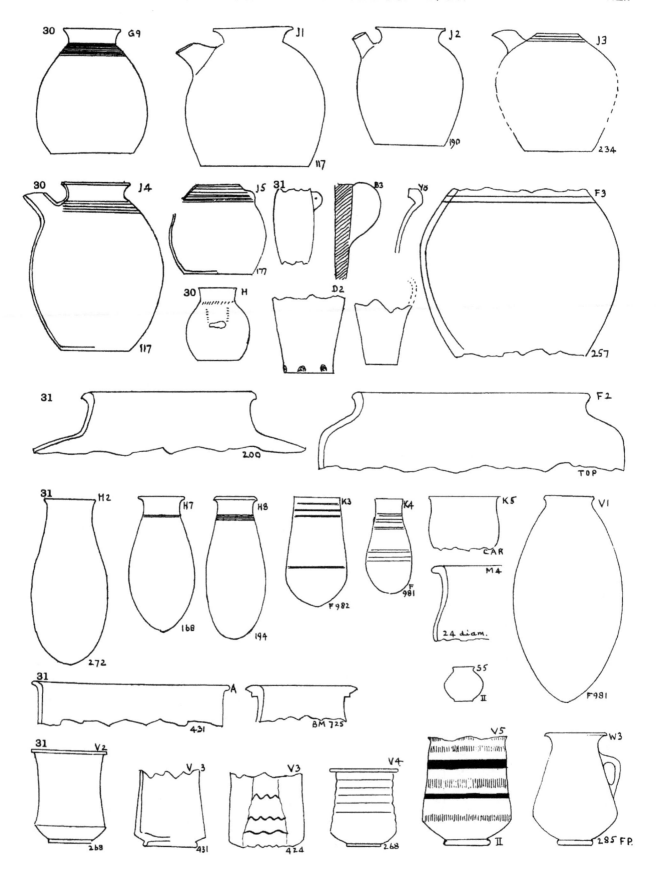

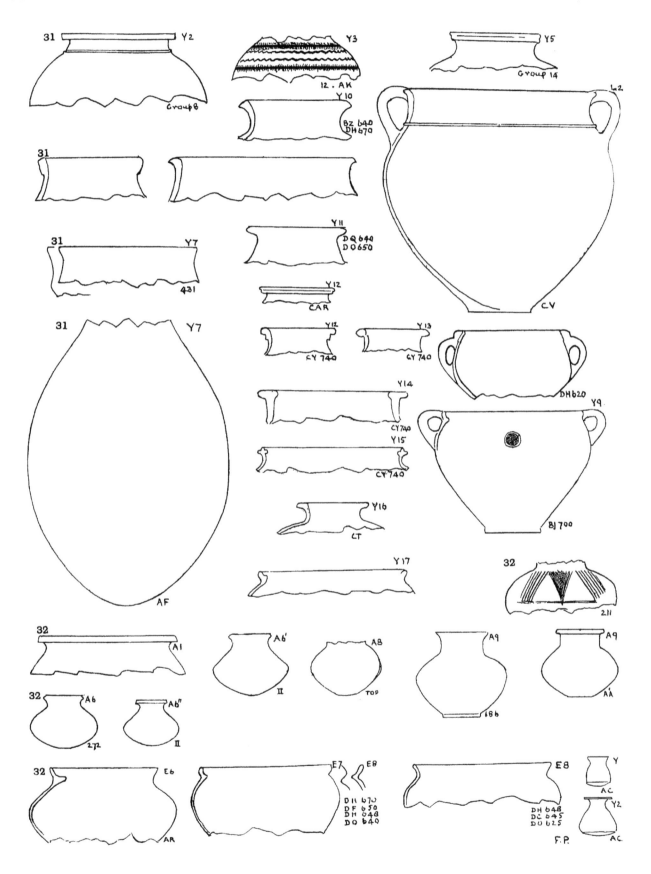

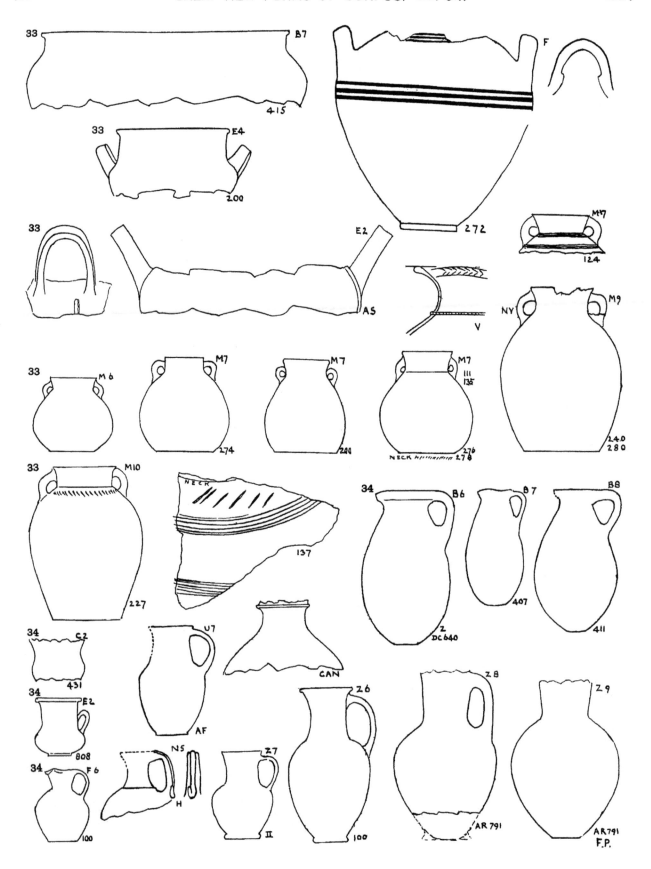

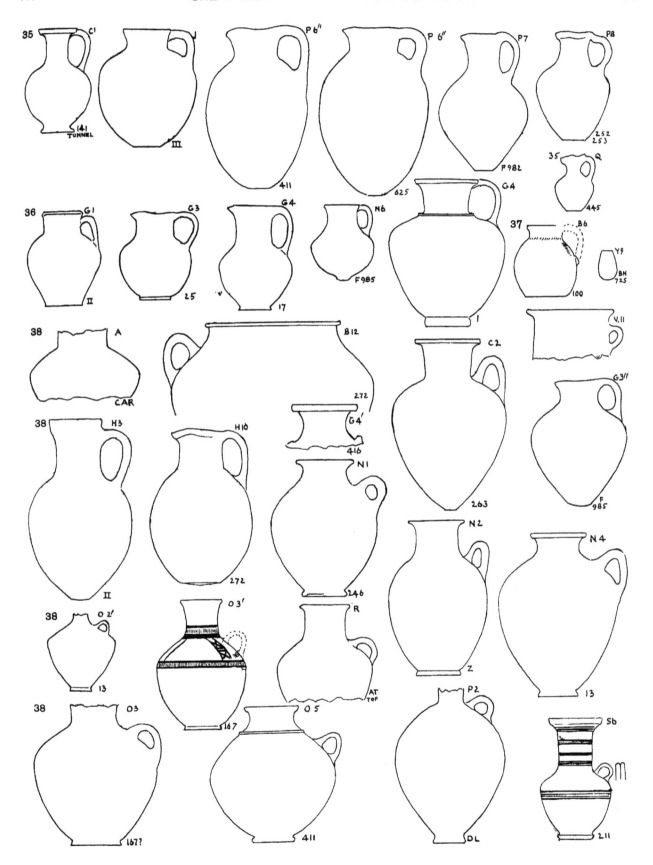

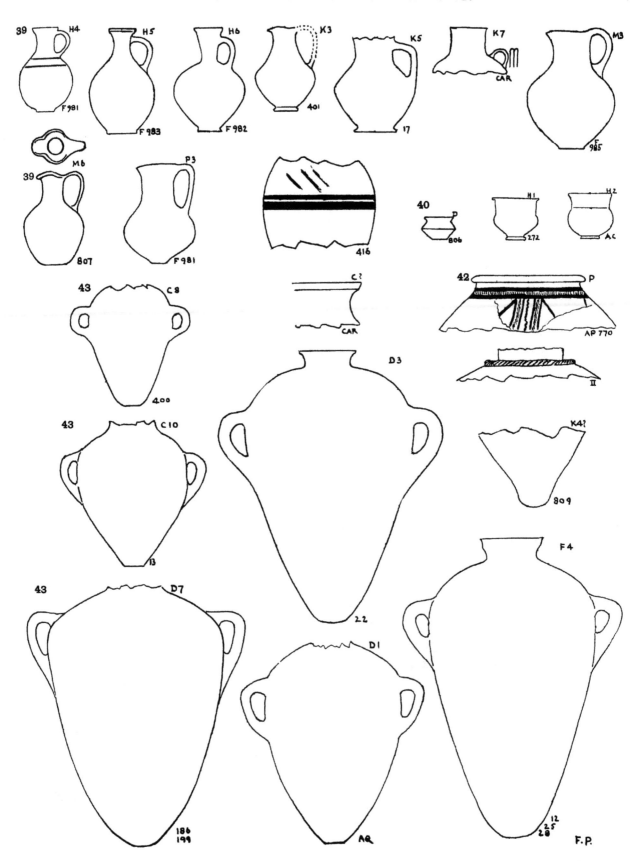

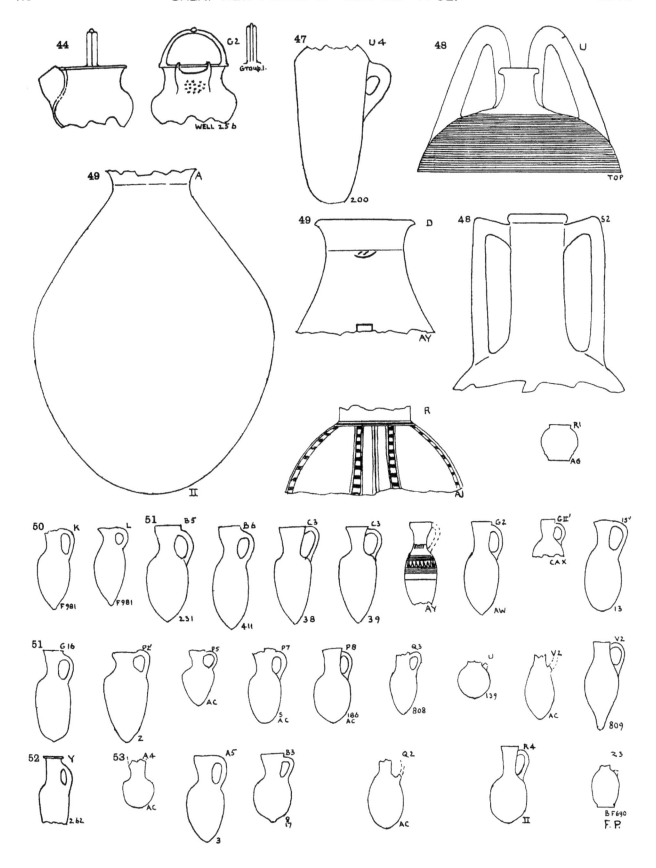

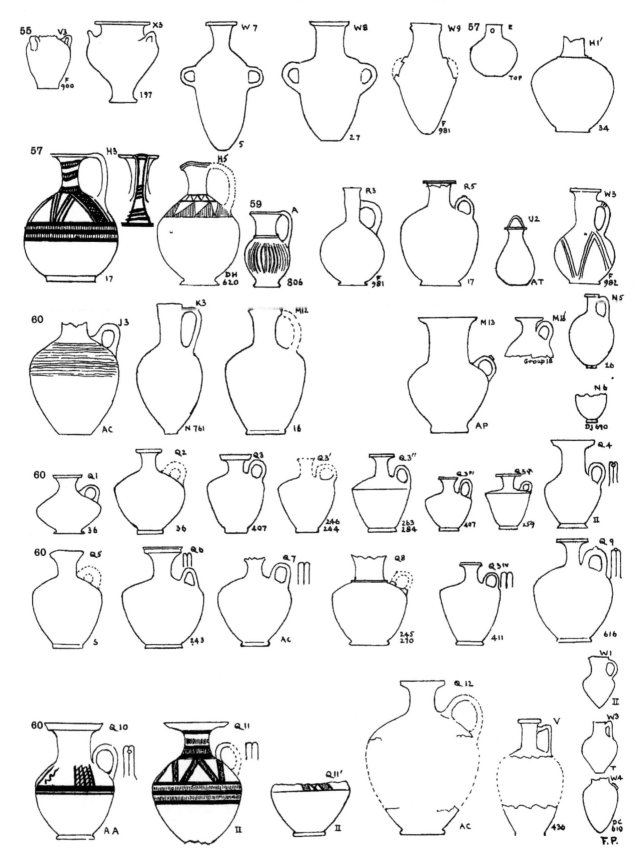

F.P.

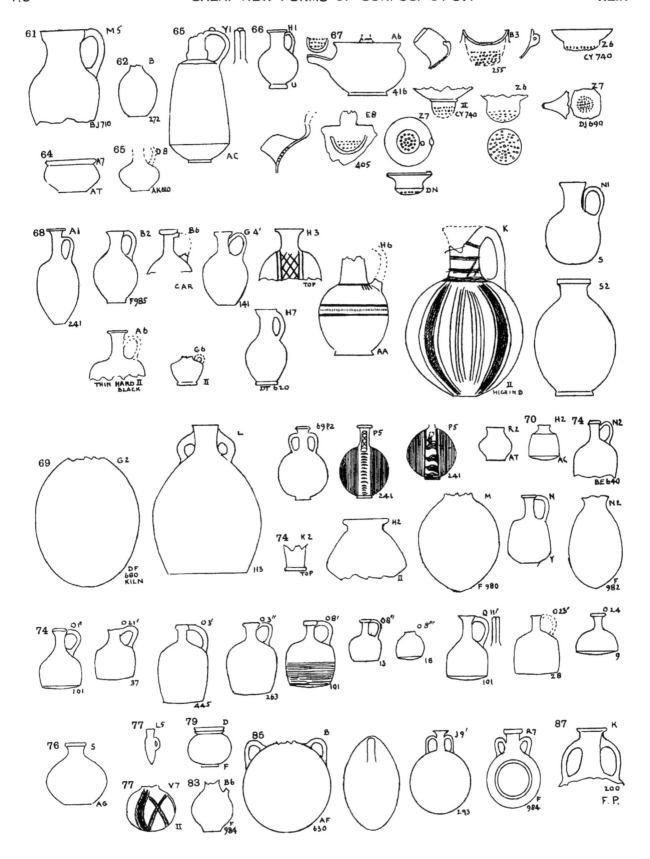

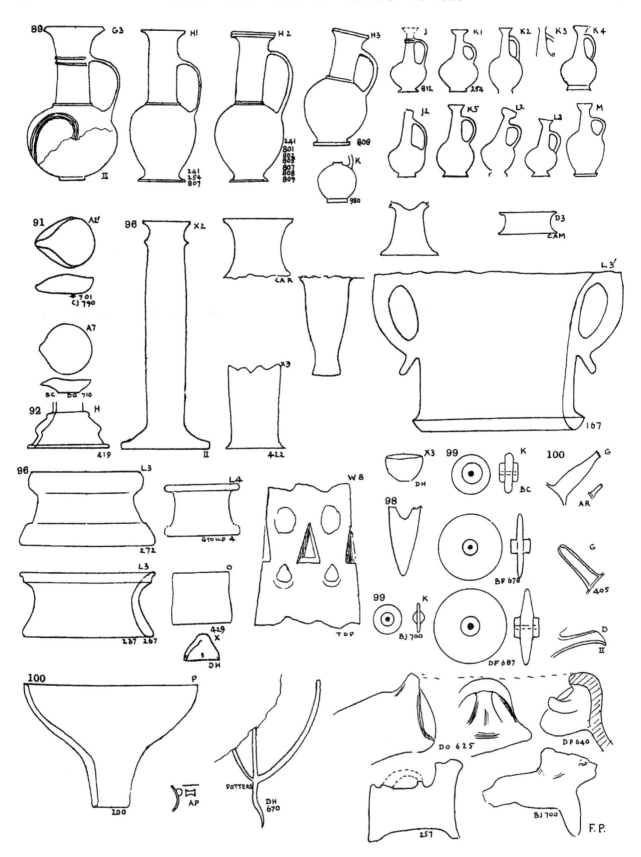

PEYEM

No.	Material					
5667	HAEMT^T	49	58.7	1/2	117.4	)(

DARIC

No.	Material					
8	HAEMT^T	494	124.5	1	124.5	X MARK X
9	BASALT	835	2569.4	20	128.5	
5670	GY.LIMST	356	6459	5	1292	)(
1	HAEMT^T	885	131.4	1	131.4	
2	JADE	AXE	66.0	1/2	132.0	AA
3	QUARTZ^T	654	6600?	50	132.0	FARA-200
4	HAEMT^T	494	663	1/2	132.6	)| MARK AW

STATER

No.	Material					
5	HAEMT^T	702	67.4	1/2	134.8	
6	GY.LIMST	373	1353.2	10	135.3	FARA
7	WT.LIMST	154	1364.8	10	136.5	

QEDET

No.	Material					
8	BK.QTZOS	8755	3428.8	25	137.1	
9	LIMESTN	916	5520	40	138.0	)(-20
5680	WT.LIMST	486	3456.1	25	138.2	
1	HAEMT^T	49	1391	10	139.1	AT -2
2	"	498	1415.1	10	141.5	Z
3	WT.LIMST	429	708.2	5	141.6	AA
4	GY.SYEN^T	12	1417.8	10	141.7	Z
5	HAEMT^T	497	4267	3	142.2	)(
6	BR.LIMST	9212	711.6	5	142.3	DJ 660
7	HAEMT^T	836	711.7	1/2	142.3	
8	"	ROUGH	723	5	144.4	
9	FLINT	406	289.3	2	144.6	
5690	BK.QTZOS	642	5866.1	40	146.7	

QEDET CONTINUED.

No.	Material					
5691	GY.LIMEST	438	734.1	5	146.8	WELL1
2	HAEMT^T	49	73.5	1/2	147.0	+ MARK
3	WT.LIMEST	2	2977.2	20	148.9	
4	WT.LIMEST	653	1490	10	149.3	-50
5	HAEMT^T	49	149.4	1	149.4	AN
6	"	49	150.1	1	150.1	AR
7	"	4875	75.1	1/2	150.2	AT
8	WT.LIMEST	494	752.6	5	150.5	
9	WT.LIMEST	15	151.6	1	151.6	- .2

NECEF

No.	Material					
5700	HAEMAT^T	49	153.1	1	153.1	AT
1	GY.LIMES	387	1539.6	10	154.0	257
2	LIMESTONE	81	3092.6	20	154.6	
3	GN.JADE?	64	155.0	1	155.0	)(-1.3
4	HAEMAT^T	651	78.6	1/2	157.2	+MARK SPRAY
5	"	49	158.0	1	158.0	AB
6	"	4875	158.8	1	158.8	AB
7	GY.SYEN^T	41	3222.0	20	161.1	200
8	HAEMAT^T	354	163.2	1	163.2	DH 620
9	WT.LIMES	55	3287	20	164.2	AY-2
5710	ALABAST^N	9207	82.7	1/2	165.4	AD
1	GY.LIMES	20	83.0	1/2	66.0	NE
2	"	20	86.5	1/2	173.0	TOP

KHOIRINE

No.	Material					
3	HAEMAT^T	49	90.5	1/2	181.0	MARK //// 257
4	GY.QTZ	656	9418.7	50	188.4	TOP

BEQA

No.	Material					
5715	WT.LIMEST	19	1897.2	10	189.7	
6	GY.QTZOS	642	9827.0	50	196.5	AK
7	HAEMATT	4875	49.8	1/4	199.2	AT
8	"	49	20.0	1/10	200.0	200
9	"	9212	200.3	1	200.3	BE 673
5720	GY.LIMEST	498	40.4	1/5	202.0	
1	CRYSTAL	494	50.8	1/4	203.2	AT
2	LIMESTON	915	203.4	1	203.4	
3	HAEMAT^T	494	203.6	1	203.6	AT
4	"	493	103.7	1/2	207.4	N-GATE
5	GY.LIMES	425	104.5	1/2	209.0	TOP
6	HAEMAT^T	49	104.5	1/2	209.0	C
7	"	49	104.8	1/2	209.6	612
8	LIMESTN	885	104.9	1/2	209.8	
9	HAEMATT	49	525	1/4	210.0	
5730	BR.LIMES	49	1053.5	5	210.7	TOP
1	HAEMAT^T	51	26.5	1/8	212.0	
2	WT.LIMES	425	53.1	1/4	212.4	
3	HAEMAT^T	41	26.9	1/8	215.2	
4	ALABAST^R	646	1088.2	5	217.6	800
5	HAEMAT^T	494	40.9	1/5	218.0	

SELA

No.	Material					
6	BK.QTZOS	83	2095.8	10	209.6	
7	HAEMAT^T	NUG	2118.8	10	211.9	)(
8	"	499	54.5	1/4	218.0	AB
9	"	695	109.5	1/2	219.0	)(
5740	BASALT	498	110.5	1/2	221.0	TOP
1	QTZ.ROCK	657	4452.8	20	222.6	

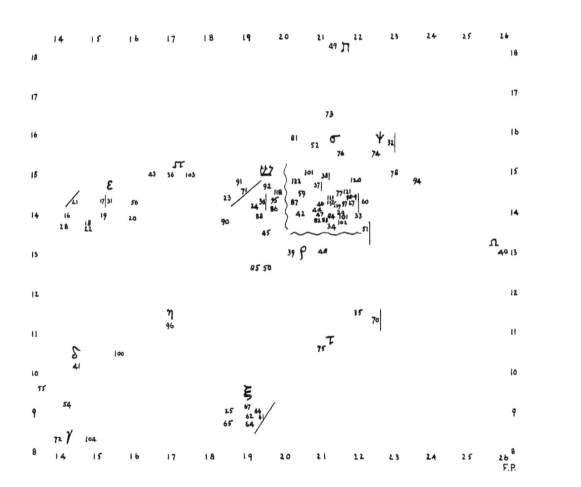

F.P.

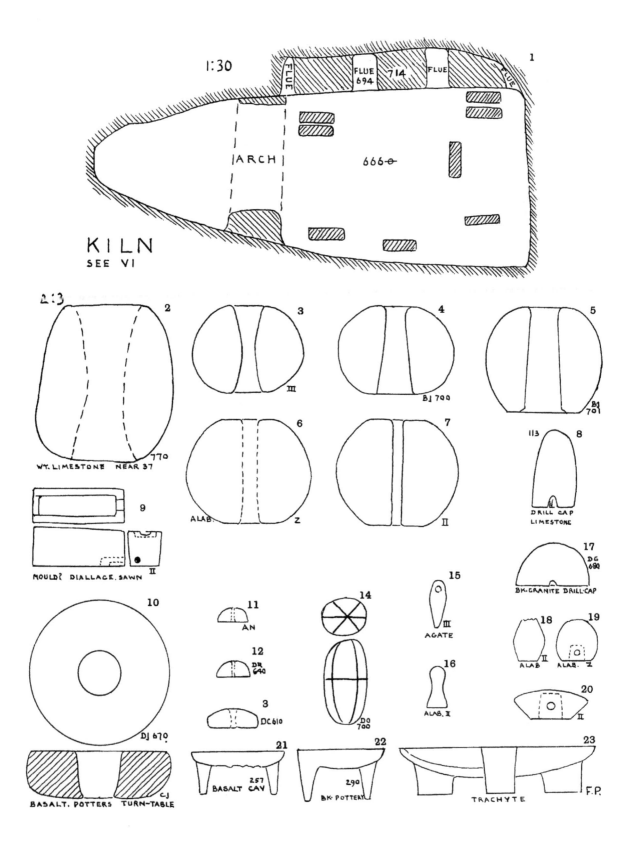

1:30

1

FLUE
FLUE
694   714   FLUE   FLUE

|ARCH|

666

KILN
SEE VI

2:3

2   770
WT. LIMESTONE   NEAR 37

3
III

4
BJ 700

5
BJ 701

6
ALAB.   Z

7
II

8   113
DRILL CAP
LIMESTONE

9
MOULD? DIALLAGE. SAWN   II

10   DJ 670
BASALT. POTTERS TURN-TABLE   CJ

11
AN

12
DR 640

3
DC 610

14

15
III
AGATE

16
ALAB. II

17   DG 690
BK. GRANITE DRILL-CAP

18   ALAB. II

19   ALAB. Z

20
II

21   257
BASALT CAV

22   290
BK. POTTERY

DO 700

23
TRACHYTE   F.P.

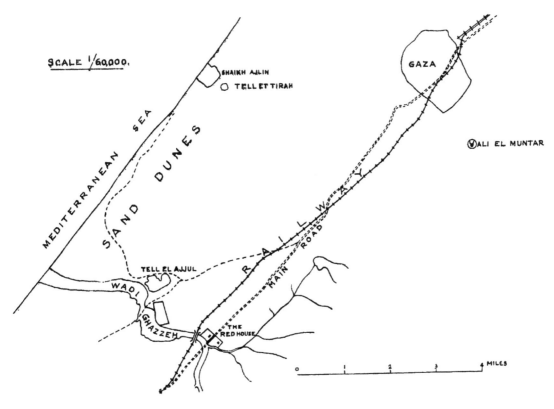

SCALE 1/60,000.

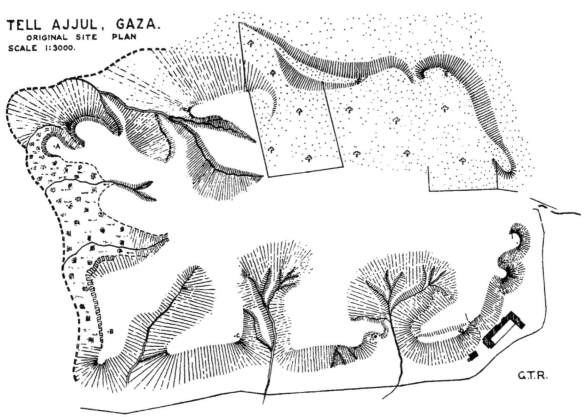

TELL AJJUL, GAZA.
ORIGINAL SITE PLAN
SCALE 1:3000.

G.T.R.

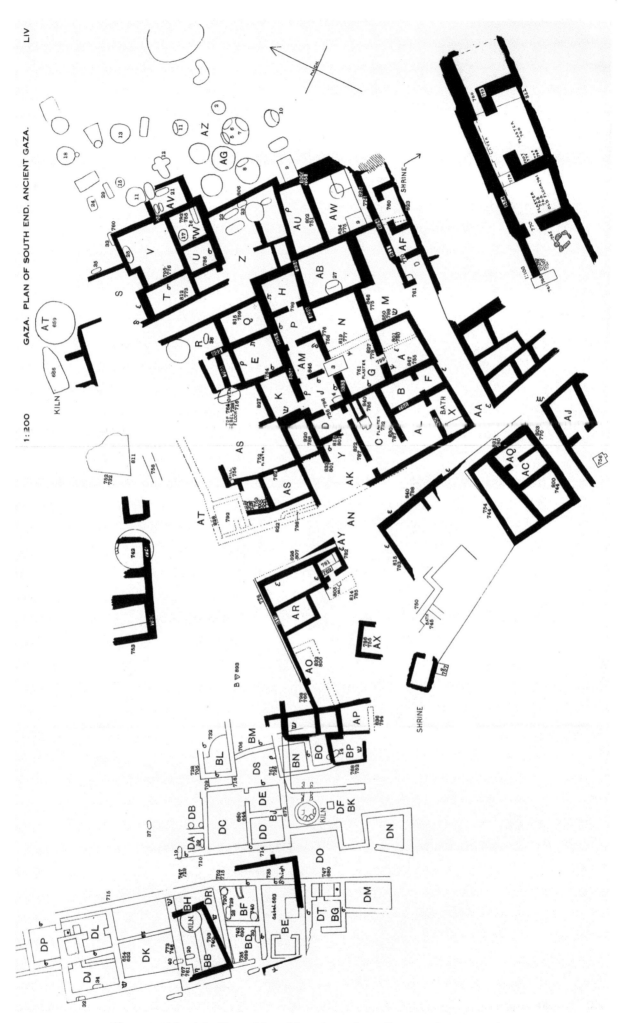

GAZA. PLAN OF SOUTH END. ANCIENT GAZA.

1:200

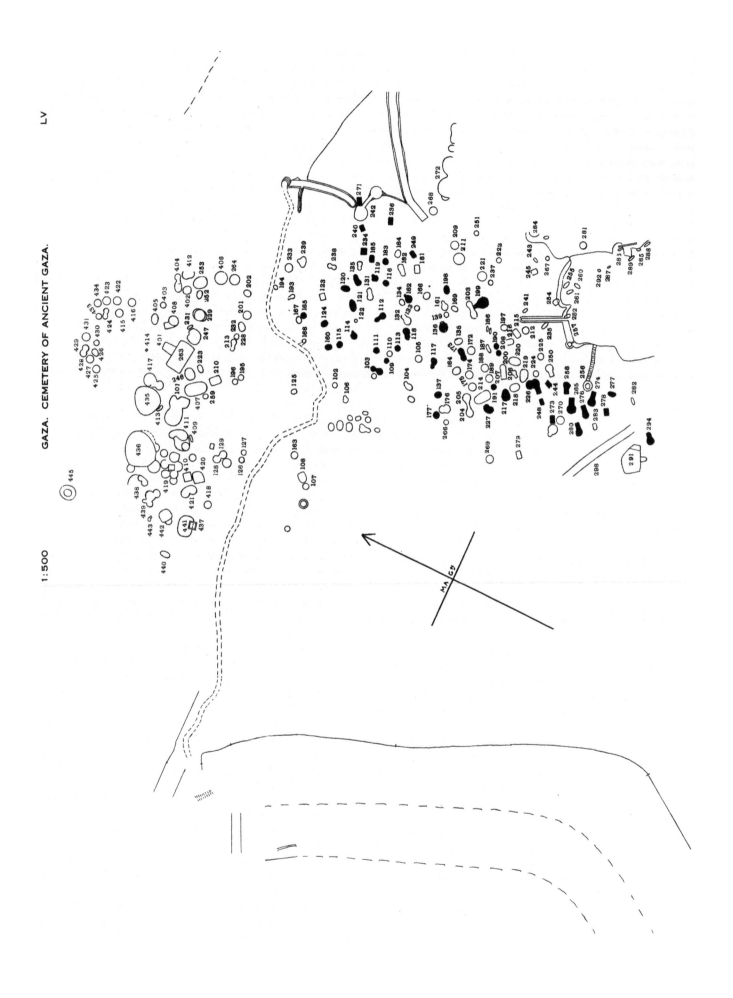

GAZA. CEMETERY OF ANCIENT GAZA.

LV

1:500

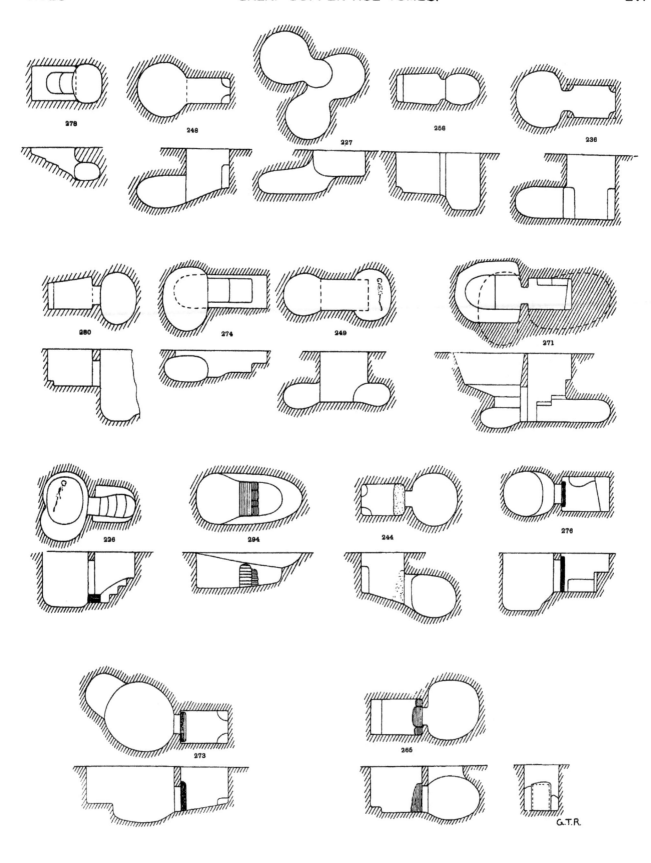

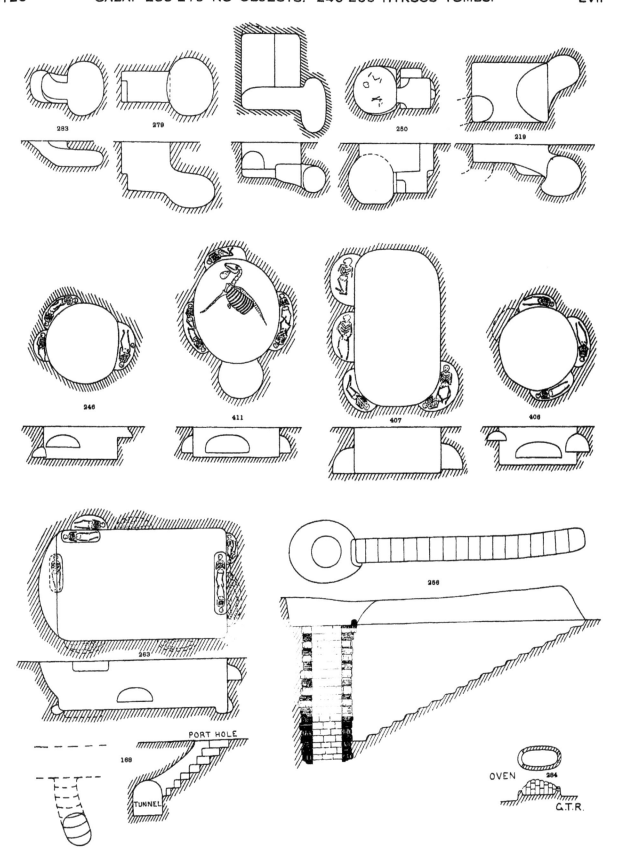

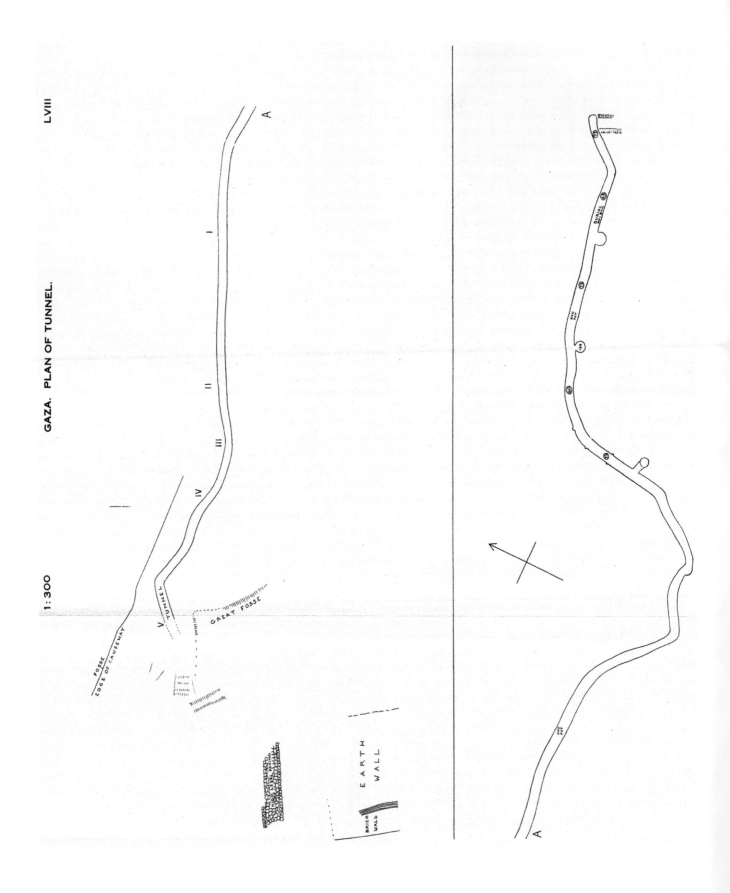

NO.	SHAFT	CHAMBER	BODY FACE HEAD	POTTERY 10Z 22N 24F 29Z 30S 30J 33M 69L	COPPER	PLACE	PLAN
103	SHALLOW	O	CONT.ᴿ	8		LONDON	φ
109	40W 36d	O	E	1		CAMBRIDGE	
111	66W 36d	D	E	4 7		JERUSALEM	
112	72W 36d E.66N 66E		E	8		"	
113	60W 35d	O	CONTᴿ	+		"	
114	24W, 60×72	O	O 6R	5 9		NEW YORK	
115	60×72	O	E 6R	1			
116	66×72 60d	O	E CON.S	2		L.	φ
117	24W 72×90	O	O	5 +			
118	47W 72×72	O	N CON.SE	1,7		L.	
119	30W 5	5b 72	O	4		BOLTON	
120	5BN 86E4½	O	O	6		ROCHDALE	
121	..	60×60 120D	O	6			
124	60×60 18D	O	O	7		L.	
135	30×45	45×60 63D	O	7		J.	
136	O	84×84,48D W S		2,4		DOOR.325°	
137	..	60×72 48 O		1,6		DOOR	
160	54×72 24	O	O	+		L.	
162	24×30 24 66×78 39		O	1			
165	65×65 18	O	E SE	4			
173	138×48 24	O	E	8			350°
177	12×36 15 60×60 48		O	2 4		L.	355°
183	66×60 60		O	3			
185	36 60 60 48 60		O	3		L.	
190		O	O	2		J.	320°
198	60 78 84 76 76 39		O	1 3		L.	
199	30 60 84 100 140 48		O	1		J.	
207	60 95 60 60 60 39		O	1			
208	60 60 72	O	O	1		L.	
217	144 84 72 33 84 19		O	1			LVI
226	66 51 78 48 60 30		S CON. E	O			LVI
227	84 132 39 90 80 36			10	XIX 49	L.	LVI
234	60 54 60	O	O	3		L.	LVI 250°
236	78 51 100 84 90 48		O	+ 4		L.	
240	72 48 70 30 36 33		O	9		L.	LVI φ 20°
244	72 48 70 75 84 66		S	4 O		L.	LVI 65°
248	72 39 84 87 78 42		O	Fb		L..	LVI 40°
249	75 48 78 {60 60 30 {60 65 39		W CON.N	2		L.	
258	72 50 65 54 48 90			5 4		C.	LVI 65°
265	54 84 72 93 84 84		N CON.E	2		DOOR φ LVI	
271	72 48 108 {66 116 30 {74 74 36		O	1 7		FITZWILLᴹ	LVI 60°
273	78 51 60 114 90 90		O	1,2			LVI 244°
274	96 48 42 72 84 18		O	5 7		L.	LVI 80°
276	78 54 60 63 72 90		N CON.E	5	275 XIX 48	L	LVI
277	30 84 12			7	XIX 46	J	340°
278	72 54 24 42 60 27		UP CON S		L	LVI 60°
280	72 45 57 80 56 12		E	2,3 9		NEWCASTLE	LVI
294	54 48 18 78 72 48			2,4	XIX 47	J	LVI DOOR
443	72 40 80 80		E CON {N {S	+			

NO.	GRAVE	BODY FACE	HEAD	POTTERY	METAL	SCARAB	BEADS	PLAN	*	PLACE
1				$18J^3$	R BAND	XIV 112				PAL. φ
2		UP	W		N TOGGLE EARRING	XIV 113	N $^{127}_{148}$			PAL. φ
3		E	N	$43A^2$ $53A^5$				J		B:
4		UP	SE	$43A$ $^{51}_{G^2}$						φ
5		E	W	$55W^7$						PAL. φ
6		UP	S	$43F$						φ
7		N	E		{ CHISEL DAGGER					φ
8										
9		N	E	$53B^3$ $^{74}_{O^3}$		XIV 114				L.
10				$16K^5 18^{23}_{KL7}$ $43E^4$			A57, H18			NY φ
11		{ E UP	N S	6^{55}_{65} $18^{11}_{K1}, 23K^{12}$ $348^6 38C^4$ $G4''$ O^3		XIV 115				N
12		{ E UP	N S	$22A' 23E'$ $43^{E3}_{G1}4$	R TOGGLE	XIV 116	ALAB XXV 33 MANY			PAL. φ
13				$18J'$ 38^{E4}_{H2} $43C^{10}$ $G15'$ $60H9''$ $O8''$	R RINGS TOGGLE	XIV 117-8				L.
14		E	N	$4A 62^3$ $89J^2$	TOGGLE			80		φ
15										
16		UP	NW	$3K'$ $60M^{89}_{O14}$	R BAND TOGGLE			W		PAL.
17		UP	{ E W	$23K^5$ $36C^4 39K^5$ $53B^3 57H^3 59A^5$	R BAND					L.
18	GRAIN PIT.			$4N^4$ $740^{4'}$			CARN. SHELL.	DA		L.
19										
20				$23G^5$ $51B^6$ $O4$ $91A'$	BONE SLIP BOX.		ALAB XXV II HOR-KA	BB		R.
21				$55W^7 60A \gamma 3', O'$	TOGGLE	XIV 119		AV		NY.
22				$18J^8$ $43E^5 51E^{11,12}$				Z		N.
23		E	N	$67'$				Z		L.
24		S	E							NY.
25		UP	N	$10E^9$ $36G^5, 38, 43F4$ $G3$		XIV 120-1				NY.
26		{ S UP	WE		TOGGLE	XIV 122		AV		
27		W CONT. S		$23K^{19} 25E'$ $43F$ $G4' 55X^8$		XIV 123	ALAB XXV. 17	AB		PAL.
28		UP	E	$18J\theta14$ $43F4$ $G4''$ $O14 24 91A$		XIV 124		BF		L.
30		UP	W	$6D^2, 9K.$ $43F$ G^{11}				BD		L.
31		UP	S	$25 G^3, 31H5, 38H5$ $43E5$ $G3$ BONE INLAY.	TOGGLE	CRYSTAL	ALAB XXV. 14			B.
32		UP	N	$43F^3$ O			ALAB XXV 9,39	DJ		PAL.
34		O						DJ		
36				$18^1_7 K1'' 25G' 342 9 38^{8}_{H1} 70$ $G^{10}_{11}1^1 60A^3 O^{99}_{24} 91A'$			ALAB. XXV. 38	R		NY
37		N	E	$O^{2'}$	RING		BRONZE SHELL	DH		NY
38				$43F^3$ C^3						
39		UP	E	$C3''$		XIII 82-3		DA		UC
40		UP	{ S N					DK		
101				43 $O1',8'',11''$		XIV 84-5				PAL. 44 φ
139	54 W STONE PIT			$23K12'$ $32A$ $51U$						L.
163	72 N			$28N^3$						L.
167	54 48 40 STONE PIT			$21B$ 38 $96L^2$		CUBIC BLOCK				PAL.
168	PORT HOLE TUNNEL			$31H^7$				LVII		
186	{66 24 10 {60 18 10			$6D^8 10E^9 19F' 23K^{17}$ $32A^9$ $43D^7 51P8$		XIV 148	XIV 89	240		L φ
187	72 24 18			$18K^7 23J'K^{16}$ $38H^2$ $G, 53$				240		NY
194	PORT HOLE TUNNEL			$31H^8$						L.
197	64 72 36 NE	N		$55X^3$ $89L$						PAL
211	120 W 20			$28M5$ $38 56$ $68A^2_4$						L.
212	60 W			$10 K^6 12H 16K^5$						PAL
221	100 W 36			$43B^6$ O'						N.
222	54 W 18			$28A'$						
223	102 54 15 N	E		$13Y^6$			ALAB XXV 24			
229	115 150 36 N	E		$51B^5$ O^{23}	TOGGLE	XXV 26				PAL.
231	78 30 18 N	E			TOGGLE			340		
235	100 36 8 UP	W		$89K$				310		N
237	54 W. 15			$96L^2$						L.
241	60 24 8			$68A' 69P' 85^3_5 89H^4$		XIV 90		135		L.
242	120 W 66			$6E^{13}$						L.
243	66 23 E	SW		$43D^6$ $P^4 60Q^6$ $91A^4$				230		N.
245	78 54 60			$60Q^8$				340		

NO.	GRAVE	BODY FACE HEAD	POTTERY	METAL	SCARAB	BEADS	PLAN	°	PLACE
246	120 W 57	LOCULI	38 N' 43 E F³ 60 Q⁸ Q'	TOGGLE	XIV 91		LVII		L. 1 φ
247	132 150 18	LOCULI	18 1⁸ 23 C⁶ 43 C' ,⁴						ASS. φ
251	48 W 39		57 89 C						
252	84 48 4	N) S) E W	35 P⁸ 43 91 A'	TOGGLE			80	L.
253	120 150 18		23 F² 35 P⁸ 51 G"	TOGGLE			305	N.
254	60 75 6	UP N	89 H' K				320	
255	30 80	UP W	67 B³		XIV 92 12 b-7		290	
256	WELL		23 K¹⁶₂₄ 38 B²				LVII	
257	WIDE PIT	O	16 KF 19 F' 23 K19 26 C' 31 F3 8 L 17 V₂ 18 H 10 52 22 N5 28 V4 N3 53 A⁴	COW 91 L³ 96 L3	TWEEZERS NEEDLES	ALA₿ XXV 31 XIV 93-5	BL. PASTE	
259	54 60 6	UP E	80 Q³⁴	TOGGLE	ALAB XXV 25			FITZ
261		UP W E N	89 N³⁴, 91 H⁴	A	XIV 128			N.Y.
263	300 170 75	UP E N L W	6 N⁶ 23 17 38 C² 43 E4 51 G² 60 Q3" 0 5" 91 A'	TOGGLE	XIV 96-7		LVII	PAL.
264	100 W 18	UP NW	18 13 43 F³ 60 H9 0 3					A.
267	66 W 45	O	16 R⁵ 96 L³					L.
268	84 W 51		31 V, V² 91 G³					
269	84 W 30	GRAIN PIT	23 W					L.
270	84 W 30		60 Q⁸					
272		OVEN { 6 C⁴ 10 K²	28 A' 31 H27 38 H16 43 C 51 06 { 68 A 51 A6 40 H" 69 B 96 L³					L.
281	78 W 42		12 C⁴ 19 C 28 A4 33 E 68 A5		XIV 129			L.
284	24 57	OVEN	13 V3 43 D³ 60 Q3"		XIV 99		LVII	L.
285	AREA		62 15 12 F 16 K5 31 W³		XIV 99		325	B.
286		UP NW	89 L					H.
289		UP N	89 L		{ PASTE FLOWER PENDANTS		300	N.Y.
292		E NW { E W	12 H 19 K³ 0 1'	TOGGLE			150	
401	66 30		17 B1 ,3' 39 C 67 E⁸ 100 G				245	L. φ
405	100 76 36	6 C4	38 B² 13 0 11'				LVII	PAL φ
406	130 W 60	LOCULI	34 B⁷ 58 { 82 43 D 51 D' 60 H9 0 11 64 19	TOGGLES	XIV 103		LVII	PAL φ
407	142 245 72	LOCULI	18 K' 43 A2' 51 G 2' F3 13 0 87 A				80	L.
408	108 126 30		10 E9 23 E9 08'		PASTE FLASK			
409	63 24 8	S E	51 G 0 8'	TOGGLE	XIV 104			
410	84 84 9	N S	23 F' 34 B⁹ 35 P 38 0³ 51 B 60 A13 0³ 89 A	TOGGLES	XIV 105		LVII	L. 64
411	84 84 9	HORSE N E L S	23 F' 34 B⁹ 35 P 38 0³ 51 B6 60 A13 0³ 89 A	TOGGLES	XIV 105		LVII	L. 64
412	95 145 30	E UP S E	0³ 13	TOGGLE	XIV 106	UZAT		PAL.
413	24 84 12	S W	23 K¹7" 38 B³				300	
414	30 30 18	O		STONE	LINED	PIT		
416	80 W 48	O	23 15 39 N³ 67 A⁶		XIV 107			L.
417	88 W 33	O	38 B² 0 11		XIV 107			
419	VARIOUS PITS	GROUP.	6 D' 92 H					
423	84 W 36	O	10 S 16 3' 19 F³ 23 K24'					
424	108 64 36	O	3 V³ 16 A 24 21 N 23 K10 32 P² 67 27 89 A					L.
429	96 W 27	O	6 C' 22 H 9 23 K24" 31 M4 96 Q 4' X 77	GRAIN	PIT			L.
434	84 W 24	O	6 C' 13 K' N5 16 K4 31 C 31 25 34 C 38 K³ 68 A E 91 G³ H, X					L.
435	265 300 30	O	19 F1² 28 21 M2 N 32 A9 89 H					
437	48 48	STONE WALLED PIT, STONE FLOOR.						
441	60 210 15	2 BODIES E W HORSE	57	TOGGLE			210	
442	140 115		6 C³ 23 K¹9					
444			38 0					
445	168 W 53	10 BODIES E N LOCULI	35 Q 38 N⁴ 43 F³ 51 6 68 L9 0³ 91 A	TOGGLE	XIV 108-11	ALAB XXV 27		PAL.
801			89 H² K		XIV 141-2			PAL.
802		O	89 H² K					
803			89 K					B
804		UP N	89 H²	KNIFE TWEEZARS	KOHL TUBE + PIN.		184	PAL.
805		UP W	12 F 19 K COW	89 H² K				M
806			40 D 59 A 89 K			+		F.
807			89 H, H²					
808			34 E² 51 Q³ 89 H², 3 L	BOWL				L.
809			39 M⁶ 43 51 V⁵ 89 H'					L
810			43 E²					
811			25 E² 43 F 51 G⁴ 91 A⁴					A

Group 1

XII DYNASTY	XV
3 K¹	
	3 X
4 F	
4 K	
4 P	
VII 6C¹ —	6C¹
VI 6C² —	6C²
IV 6C³	
XI 6C⁴ —	II 6C⁴
	II 6C⁶
	6C6'
6C7	
	6C8
III 6D¹ —	6D¹
	6D³
6E³	
	6E4
	6E14
6M	
6N?	
6N5	
6N7	
	7E
	9F¹
10E4	
	10E9
	10N2
10K8'	
10K9	
	10V
	12G³
12G4	
II 12G5	
	12M8
	12N6
13E	
	13T³
	13V7
13Y6	
13Y11	
15G —	15G
	15H²
15H3	
15M³	
15P9	
15R	
15U4	
16K3	
II 16K4	
16K6	
	16R³
16T4	
	17B
17B1'	

Group 2

XII	XV
	17B³
II 17B4 —	17B4
17V2	
	17V4
18F2	
	II 18J4
	18J6
IV 18J7 —	18J7
III 18J8	
18J11	
18J12	
IV 18J13	
18J14 —	18J14
18K1	
	18K1'
18P2	
18P5	
19F	
	III 19F¹
	19F²
19R	
	19S
19S²	
20L'	
	20N
21A	
21A³	
	21B
21B'	
	21V
21X —	21X
	22J8
22N5	
23B2	
23B4	
23B9	
23C¹	
23C4	
IV 23D	
	II 23D²
23E8	
23E10	
	23E25''
III 23G4	
23J1	
23J2	
23J5	
	23K³
23K9	
II 23K10 —	23K10
23K12	
	23K16
III 23K17 —	II 23K17
II 23K18	

Group 3

XII	XV
23K18'	
III 23K19 —	IV 23K19
23K19'' —	23K19''
23K20	
	II 23K22
II 23K22'	
23K22'' —	23K22''
II 23K24	
III 23K24''	
23K25	
II 23K25' —	23K25'
II 23K25''	
II 23K25'''	
23P4	
23R	
	23V2
	23Z3
25B	
	25E2
	25G'
26B3	
II 26C	
II 26C²	
26E	
	26Y
28A¹ —	28A¹
28A²	
28A³	
II 28A4	
28C	
28G²	
	28H5
28M12	
28N²	
	28O²
28Y²	
31K5	
	31V
II 31V2	
31V3	
31V5	
31Y¹	
	31Y2
31Y4	
31Y7	
	31Y8
V 31Y10	
31Y16	
32A7	
32A8	
	32A9
32E5	
V 32E7	
VII 32E8 —	32E8

Group 4

XII	XV
32 N	
32 S4	
	32Y
	32Y2
33C	
	33E²
34 B¹	
34B6 —	34B6
	34E²
34T³	
	34V7
34Z6	
	34Z8
	34Z8'
	34Z9
38A —	38A
	38B
	38C²
38H5	
	38N²
	38O5
38P2	
	40H2
	42P
43A¹	
II 43A²	
43A8	
43C²	
43C³	
43F³ —	43F³
	43D¹
	49R
	49R¹
	57G²
V 51G3	
51G4	
51G8	
51G11 —	51G11
	51G12
51G15	
	51P2'
	51P5
III 51P7	
	51P8
	51V2
	53A¹
	53A4
	53Q²
53Z3	
57H5	
	57E
	60H11
	60H13
	60H15

Group 5

XII	XV
	60K³
60N6	II 60M13
	60Q3'''
60Q3IV	
	60Q4
	60Q11
	60W4
61M5 —	61M5
	63K
65C	
	65D8
	65N7
	65Y¹
	66H¹
67Z7	
	68A
	68A6
68B6	
68G7	
	68N¹
73B	
	74H²
	74N
74N2	
	74O0''
	74O1 — 74O1
74O1'	
III 74O3	
74O8	
	74O14
II 74O15	
74O20	
	74O21
74P3	
	76S
	85B
89A —	89A
II 91A¹ —	V 91A¹
91A²	
91A2'	
II 91A3 —	91A3
96D³	
96K³	
IV 99K	

```
157 TYPES 130
    TOTAL 261
    IN COMMON
        26
131 PECULIAR 104
ROMAN NUMERALS
PREFIXED STATE
NUMBER OF EXAMPLES
```

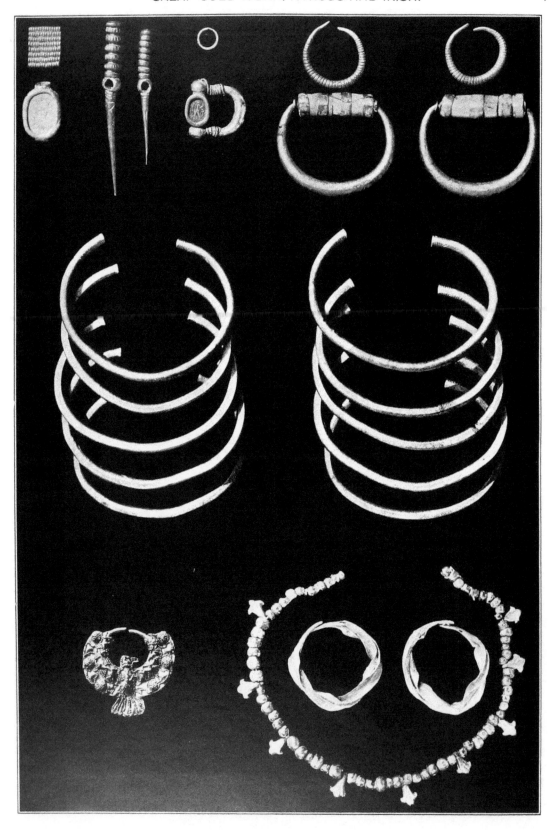

BRITISH SCHOOL OF ARCHAEOLOGY IN EGYPT

ANCIENT GAZA
II
TELL EL AJJŪL

BY

FLINDERS PETRIE, Kt., F.R.S., F.B.A.

LONDON
BRITISH SCHOOL OF ARCHAEOLOGY IN EGYPT
UNIVERSITY COLLEGE, GOWER ST., W.C.1
AND
BERNARD QUARITCH
11 GRAFTON ST., NEW BOND ST., W.1
1932

PRINTED IN GREAT BRITAIN
BY HAZELL, WATSON AND VINEY, LTD.
LONDON AND AYLESBURY

CONTENTS

LIST OF PLATES

STAGES OF EARLY PALESTINE

		Egyptian Date.
Handled cup, Teleilet Ghassul pottery	. . . . .	S.D. 30 ?
Ledge handles begin, fine neolithic .	. . . .	S.D. 40
Copper users eject neolithics .	. . . .	S.D. 60

	Dyn.	B.C.
Copper Age cemetery, Tell el Ajjul	V–VI	3300–3100
Ledge handles disappear	VI	3300 ?
Palace I built (before vii dyn.)	end VI	3200
Conquest of Egypt	VII	3127
Ejection from Egypt	end VIII	2912
Great denudation . , ...	.	3000–2600 ?
Courtyard cemetery, veined dagger	X–XI	2800–2600
Palace II built, Egyptian	XII	2500
Palace III Hyksos (before xv dyn.)	XV	2400
Palace IV Hyksos	XVI	2100
Palace V Egyptian	XVIII	1500
Latest tomb	XXII	900

Financial difficulties continue to surround most of our subscribers, and the receipts of the School have been greatly diminished. It is hoped that all who cannot afford the usual donation will raise contributions to an equal amount and send them in.

ANCIENT GAZA II

CHAPTER I

THE HISTORICAL POSITION

1. THE general conditions of the site of Tell el Ajjūl have been already described in the previous volume, sections 1 to 7. Most of the former staff were present during last season. Others who joined us were Mr. T. P. O'Brien, Lt.-Col. N. P. Clarke, Mr. and Mrs. Warren Hastings, Dr. Sperrin-Johnson, and, part of the time, Miss Bentwich.

2. The purpose of work last season was the recovery of the public buildings, and the further examination of the cemetery. Looking at our experience at Gerar and Beth-pelet, the important buildings were likely to be on the highest part of the Tell, nearest to the sea, to secure the cooler breeze. On beginning a wide clearance there, we soon found walls 4 ft. thick, of large square buildings. Toward the north were smaller irregular buildings, which led to nothing. Our clearance was spread southwards, as far as the larger walls extended. Having found the length of frontage, the work was then widened eastward, as much as the time allowed in one season. In any case we went down to the basal marl over this area, so as to have a complete history of the region which we cleared. This is a necessary rule, in order to obtain the historical relations of the remains.

The broad result was the discovery of the massive lower courses of five successive buildings, one under the other, about 4 ft. apart in level. Each was a definite block of rooms, self-contained (see plan, pl. xxvi). The lower blocks have bathrooms, white plastered, with sloping floor. This proves that these buildings were for residence as palaces, and were not temples.

3. The dating of these palaces is limited in both directions. The lowest palace, I, has fragments of pottery similar in nature to those of later levels ; but not a single fragment or form is like those of the Copper Age, found in 1931 (*Gaza I*, xli) and also in the cemetery again this year. This delimits the palace as subsequent to the Copper Age, which I dated last year early in the vith dynasty (*G.* I, p. 3). Another apparent indication of age is the massive sandstone foundation of palace I ; the supply of over 1,000 tons of hewn stone can only have come from the excavation of the great fosse around three sides of the hill. This fosse is of the North Syrian type, vertical on the outer side and with a long slope up the hill on the inner face, like the fortification of Homs, Emesa. We know that the viith and viiith dynasties of Egypt came from North Syria, and presumably the great fosse was cut by these people, at the latter part of the vith dynasty, when on their way into Egypt. After they conquered southward they would not have any object in fortifying Gaza so strongly ; the only use of such strength was while it was a frontier city. Thus the building of palace I is limited to the period before the close of the Egyptian vith dynasty.

4. At the other end of the scale, the last palace is associated with pottery of the xviiith dynasty, especially a piece of a jar with double cartouches of Hatshepsut and Tehutmes III, 1481 B.C. (viii, 117). Not a scarab or other object of the xixth dynasty was found in the palace region, so probably the latest building was due to Tehutmes III, and its fall to the revolt under Akhenaten. Since that time the only occupants have been Arab squatters.

5. There are, then, three palace buildings, II, III and IV, between palace I late in the vith dynasty and No. V at 1480 B.C. There was a long interval of erosion between I and II, during which 30 inches of blown and washed earth covered the ashes of ruin, corresponding to the period of desolation, described in *G* I, sect. 13. This pushes the date of palace II some centuries after the vith dynasty ; as that building is of very fine work, it is likely to be of the xiith dynasty, and the interval of six centuries between the founding of I and II is quite probable.

The walls of palace II were taken down for bricks to build palace III, so it had no long existence, and the substitution of a massive fortress in place of the palace II would accord with the Hyksos xvth = xiiith dynasty in Egypt.   Palace IV was in the Hyksos age, as the horse sacrifice and horse feast were held at its foundation ; it would, therefore, be the work of the Hyksos xvith dynasty.   This historical distribution seems therefore fairly fixed, by its concordance with known history.

Most of the drawings are not signed, as there was a continual mixture of work, due to the various hands, Miss Bentwich, Miss Tufnell, Col. Clarke, Mr. Harding, and myself.

It was a season in which more than the usual amount of energy had to be expended.   We were working on a large scale, and Lady Petrie and I were fully occupied in keeping things running. Superintendence at every point is always needed to ensure a successful expedition.

We hope, if donations are forthcoming, to find the temple site next, in order to gain further evidence as to the dating.   Lady Petrie's work of collecting sufficient funds was rendered so difficult by the financial situation, that it was found necessary to employ capital reserves to a large extent.   There had been outlay with a view to co-operation with U.S.A. (as in the previous season when New York had borne one fourth of the costs).   At the beginning of the work, however, it became apparent that no help would come from U.S.A.   With one exception, the larger donors at home were unable to give.   Sir Charles Marston, now Vice-Chairman of the School, was alone in sending a major contribution.

CHAPTER II
THE COPPER AGE

6. A WIDE search was made in the plain below the city, for more remains of the Copper Age.   From the cemetery known last year on the eastern side, the ground was turned over along the north and west of the city, but no such early graves were found till near the close of the season.   This cemetery was about a quarter of a mile west of the city, with some forty graves, half of which contained copper daggers, see pl. lix, Register of tombs 1530–1572.

7. There were three types of tomb : A, lined pits ; B, shaft, and chamber on south ; C, shaft, and chamber on north, pls. l, li.

Type A.   A rectangular pit was dug in the marl, and lined with a wall of upright slabs, or of loose

blocks of stone.   Over this was a roofing of blocks, which had invariably collapsed.   The burials were always contracted, with the thighs at less than a right angle to the spine.   The head was to the east in all types of Copper Age tombs, but the face might be to north or south according to the direction of the chamber, in order to face the shaft.

Type B.   Here there is a square shaft, and the chamber is a shallow recess, on the south side just sufficient for the body, usually 20 to 30 ins. high.

Type C.   The chamber is on the north of the shaft, and usually wider than the shaft.

8. The forms of the daggers (pls. ix–xiii) vary from a smooth curved face, as fig. 50, to a stiletto-like spine with a blade on each side as thin as card, fig. 67.   The type is not connected with any form of tomb.   The only feature connected with the tomb is the handle, of which traces are seen at the butt ; this in some cases extends along the edges of the butt (figs. 50, 52, 57, 64, 66, 67) and these are all in the B tombs.   It is very unusual in other countries to have the riveting so prolonged on the sides of the butt.

The pottery is always of thin friable light-brown ware poorly baked (pl. xxix, 30 F to J).   The form is always flat-based, a tall globular body, with narrow neck.   In the B tombs there are a few jars of taller and better form, with high neck, and no ledge handle, and only one jar in six has a spout. In C tombs there are four jars in all, and each with a spout (xxi, 10).

9. In the west cemetery, near the Tell, a pit (1511) was found containing fragments of various domestic forms of Copper Age pottery.   These are at the base of pl. xxxvi.   The hole-mouth jar, 2, and the flat bases, 4, 5, are typical of the time.   The row of thumb-bosses on 5 is a frequent ornament on the early pottery of the Copper Age.   The pan, 1, with turned-in edge, seems to have led on to the pans of the courtyard cemetery, 1400, which are probably of the x–xith dynasties ; this is the only Copper Age type which survived the North Syrian attack.   Otherwise the whole of the forms and ware of this pottery, and the forms of dagger, entirely disappeared at the entry of the North Syrian people.

CHAPTER III
THE EARLIEST PALACE

10. THE cutting of the great fosse around three sides of the hill on which the city was built, supplied an immense amount of stone. This is a soft sand-stone of dune origin, infiltrated by gypsum. In all lands where the evaporation exceeds the rainfall—as in Egypt and south Palestine—there will be an accumulation of salts owing to the capillary rising of moisture from below. This brings gypsum to the surface in Palestine, and slowly concretes the sand dunes. The stone is easy to cut, and was worked out in slabs about 30 inches across and 6 to 9 inches thick. These were used for the lowest course of palace I (xliii, xlv). They were placed on edge for the inner and outer faces of the wall, and then the space between was filled in with rougher blocks, as shown in the plan. The portions as yet exposed are drawn in detail, which will be completed when the later walls over it are removed.

11. The stone slabs are carefully dressed with flat edges, and the smooth face is slightly drafted along the margin. This base course was about half sunk in the native marl, and half projected above the paving level, forming a wainscot of stone, on which rested the wall of mud-brick.

One drum of a stone column remained, half covered by a wall of palace II (xliv, 3). Where it originally stood may be discovered when the later buildings are removed.

Regarding the plan, xlv, as a whole, there are five chambers on the north side, as far as preserved, but the east end has been entirely removed for stone. It can hardly be doubted that there was a return wing on the south ; if so, there would have been at least eight chambers along the west side. The south and east sides of the courtyard have still to be opened up.

12. Dimensions. Along the west wall there were doubtless rooms as on the north. As the cross-walls are 45 inches thick, like those on the north, it is evident that we have not yet reached the south side. There must be a wall at MV not yet found, agreeing with that at MW, and so the south side will be beyond MW, making the west side 150 feet long. Similarly the north side must be at least 75 feet long. Until the plan is ascertained the unit of measure is uncertain, but it seems likely to be the foot of 11.7 inches, formed from the best known early digit and widely used.

13. In the north-west corner of the palace is a bathroom (xliv, 1) paved with white plaster, sloping down 10 inches from the north-east to the south-west corner, where probably a drain ran out through the back wall, now destroyed. In the view, the two plastered steps in the doorway, leading up to the bath, are at the right hand, with a large jar partly sunk in the ground. The stone wall leading thence to the left, is the base from which most of the brick wall is removed, to show the construction. Backing on this wall is a pit in the bathroom floor, which was probably a cess-pit.

In OG (xlv) there is part of a plastered floor remaining.

14. Levels are on the plan, in inches over sea level ; they are fixed from the government bench mark on the top of the hill. The native marl is highest at the north of the palace, about 970 ; at the palace it sloped down to 950 at the north wall, 930 at OG, and still lower to the south. The stone foundations were half sunk in the marl ; the tops of the edge slabs vary from 968 at the north to 936 at the south, sloping 1 in 44. The floor of the bath-room is raised to 975, to drain down to 965, the same as the step up to the bath, 964. The plaster floor at OG is at 939.

15. Outside palace I, on the north of it, are remains of a stone revetment, xliv, 2. This was a facing to a bank of sandstone grit (on the right) that was crowned by the city wall. At the foot of this slope was a paved way, seen brightly here in reflected sunlight. The level of this is 1,000, so that it was the same as the door and sill of palace II (999). As there is only a foot of loose earth, however, between the stone and the native marl, and the great wall base would probably be somewhat raised, it seems more likely that the revetment was con-nected with palace I, the nearest floor of that being at 975.

16. The bank of clean sandstone grit would be obviously supplied by all the digging of the fosse, and trimming the blocks there quarried ; it would therefore be co-eval with the fosse which supplied the stone for palace I. On the top of the bank origin-ally stood the city wall of black mud brick. It has long ago been washed away by the rains, but it left its evidence in a slope of mud wash on the inner side of the bank. This was seen at a level of 1087, sloping down at 27° to 970 level, in a pit which we sank about 60 ft. south of the remains of the revetment. This mud was clearly washed down, and not a tip heap, as there were long thin streaks of mud and sand alternating down the whole length exposed. It doubtless continued below 970, but to expose the whole of the bank face would require a heavy removal of earth.

CHAPTER IV

PALACES II, III, IV AND V

17. PALACE I was ruined and burnt, leaving a bed of ashes nearly six inches thick over its ruins. Some centuries elapsed, during which there was heavy rainfall. This denuded the land seven feet or more in parts, washing away the whole height of the tunnel and roof (G. I, 11), and it was therefore subsequent to the formation of the fosse and defences. It also washed away the Copper Age tombs in some parts.

Such rainfall spread about three feet of washed earth over the ashes of palace I, and it was on this plain of earth that palace II was built. Probably the builders never saw more than some mouldering lines of brick wall on this surface, and they did not use a single wall of the old construction as a basis.

18. Palace II (xlvi) was entirely built of fine yellow clay bricks, hard and durable, mostly 14 inches square, and some 14 × 22 inches. These made up 39 inches of wall thickness by leaving a wide middle joint in the mass. These were the thinnest walls of all the palaces, an evidence of a sense of power and security quite different from that shown by the 6 ft. wall of palace I, or the 8½ ft. wall of palace III. This security points to palace II being the work of the powerful xiith dynasty, the most settled of all periods between the vth and xviiith dynasties.

The bathroom is on the east side (xliv, 4), with a drain of stone, under the courtyard of that age. The bathroom floor is of white plaster, sloping down to the drain-hole in the wall. On the south side of the room was the cesspit. There had evidently been a stone seat here, as the marks of it remain. Such a seat block (from some other position) is seen in xliii, 1 lying tilted against the corner of the brick tower, to the left of the levelling rod. In the pit were some sherds of fine pottery, both hard white and thin brown Cypriote bowls.

19. The walls had deep foundations, 20 ins. along the front. They had been carefully taken to pieces, and the stepping seen in the view is due to the removal of regular courses of bricks. This was done by the builders of palace III, the Hyksos, in order to re-use the bricks. In sections cut in this later wall, the yellow bricks are in alternate layers with the black bricks.

The north-east corner of palace II has been entirely destroyed. The front wall is in good state below the floor level, for 20 ins. deep. The entrance is marked by the large irregular flagstones placed for a threshold.

20. Dimensions. The front is 785 inches, the depth back about 482 to 496, but the outside of the back has not yet been exposed. The outer walls are 39 thick, made up of 14 + 22, and 3 of the same yellow clay filled in between. The basis of the planning is the foot of 13 inches; front 785 is 60 of 13.08, divided into rooms of 8, 7½, 19, and 10 feet; the depth inside is 40 feet, with rooms of 11, 9½, and 6 feet. The mean foot is 13.28 inches; this is the Great Northern foot, which was used from the Indus to England, and from Germany to Egypt.

21. Palace III was built while the previous palace was in good condition, so that the sound material could be re-used. The thickness of the walls suggests that this preceded the close of the xiith dynasty, as such defence would have been useless when the Hyksos held Egypt as well as Palestine. That they ruled both countries in one government is proved by the High Treasurer, Ha-al, holding the same office in both lands, even late in the dynasty. The plastered walls of palace III are seen in xliii, 2, bearing many coats of renewal. The nearest corner of the buttress in the foreground has a broken edge of brick which shows traces of having been a projection, so that may have been the side of a doorway, with the usual reveal cut away. The floor is so much denuded that no trace of an opposite pier could be found. Pl. xlviii.

22. For some reason the whole of the back wall began to tilt inward, probably due to some sinking of foundation over looser earth in the old rooms: there is sometimes five inches or more of overhang. This led to partial reconstruction of more than one date. The complex of walls in chamber MU is shown in the view, xliii, 3. The lowest level marked 1 is top and base at 970/966, 2 is at 990/968, running on to 3 996/990; 4 is part of the yellow brick palace II 996/976; 5 is the 8 ft. Hyksos wall 1088/991, made out of 4; 6 is a later cross-wall 1051/994, and 7 is the subsequent thickening of the back-wall 1053/994, to strengthen it against the inward tilt. The meaning of the separate block under 7 is not yet clear till 7 is removed.

Under the north-west corner of the palace was found a globular jar, with a saucer covering it; there were small bones in it. The level of it was 986, the wall foundation being 1021 to 1033. A bust (pl. v) from these levels is probably of Hyksos type.

23. Palace IV was a refurbishing of palace III. The leaning back-wall was held back by thickening it with a lining, and by taking down some cross-walls and putting in others thicker, to take the thrust. The floor was raised five feet on the new walls. In xliii, 2 a wall that has been mostly taken down is in the middle distance, left in stepping courses. The new lining wall had covered the old plastered face for five feet up, and so preserved it. At the left hand there is, just showing, a portion of the thick new wall which buttressed the back-wall on the right. Part has been cut away, with the lining wall, in our excavations, in order to examine the structure. The exact order of various changes can hardly be settled, but the purpose was evidently to hold up the overhanging back-wall and raise the floors. Pl. xlix.

At this refounding of the palace at the higher level, a pit about five feet deep was dug in the debris and in the wall of a building north of palace III. In this pit was thrown a sacrificed horse, after removing the shoulder blades for food ; on the ground by the pit were strewn the bones of two horses, completely separated, evidently the remains of a horse feast, see pl. lii. This will not accord with any position in the history except the xvith dynasty.

24. Palace V was almost all washed away by denudation. The builders utilised palace IV, raising the floors and extending the buildings farther west. In each period the builders seem to have pushed the building area westward, by banking up more sand-stone grit on the outer side of the city. Of the new buildings of palace V there is nowhere more than a foot left, and the walls thin out so that, after tracing an inch or two of brick to the north, they vanish, probably much before the original end of the building.

25. The only later occupation was by Arab squatters. Much denudation had sloped the ground, so that there was an exposure of some of the earlier strata. Thus Arab objects are found at various date levels on the surface. More serious mixture was caused by the innumerable grain pits sunk by the Arabs, and afterwards filled up as rubbish holes. The digging of these had thrown up earlier material and so brought objects upward, while it let late things fall down below. Hence in judging of the range of any kind of pottery or other objects, it is only a continuity of occurrence which is decisive, while single examples at very different levels may be regarded as sporadic. Of course so soon as a

rubbish pit was found, all work around it was stopped and the whole contents were completely brought to the top. There anything notable was kept, and the rest removed before cutting away the ground around the pit. After taking these precautions, it was found that the whole area of the palaces and courtyard was truly level within a foot, except for later changes, as stated in the chapter on Decorated Pottery. The only traces of construction in Arab times are a few rude lines of rough stones of walls skew to the xviiith dynasty walls which they overlay.

26. In connection with the palaces should be noted the burials in the courtyard. A few were at the Hyksos level, but were not of importance. The bones were measured, the skulls were waxed in the field. In the store room they were immersed in melted wax for a time, to soak in and expel the air. When cold they were completely swathed in a tight strip of muslin, and finally waxed to secure this binding. Nothing short of this will preserve, in transport, skulls full of earth such as these. The skulls have been placed in the collection of crania, Eugenics Department, University College.

Below these Hyksos bodies were other burials, which must have preceded the xiith dynasty, judging from their depth under the courtyard, and from the pottery found with them. Those in the north of the court (pl. xliv) may perhaps be rather earlier than those to the south (pl. xlv), but the pottery scarcely differed. The forms 25 E to G and 28 P (pl. xxviii) are unlike any found in Hyksos tombs or in palace II. They seem to belong to x–xith dynasties, and it was in that period that the place was deserted, and liable to be used as a cemetery. A veined bronze dagger (ix; xiv, 74) was found with burial 1417, and is the earliest known of this type. A donkey was buried at the mouth of the tomb, similar to the favourite donkeys buried by the tomb of a noble in the Ist dynasty (*Tarkhan* II, xix).

CHAPTER V

METAL WORK

27. In the open courtyard before the palace there stood a brick tower, numbered 1450 on pl. xlviii. There was a height of about five feet remaining, and evidently it had been greatly denuded like the palace buildings. There was no doorway, but within it was a chamber 68 × 58 inches, the tower being 184N, 183S, 174W, 171 ? E. ins. The paving of rough stones in the chamber was at 1018 level. Adjoining the north end of the east side of the tower there lay a jar containing burnt bones of bird and gazelle : this was lower than the base of the tower, so it might belong entirely to an older period. The floor of the chamber, 1018 level, agrees with that of the adjacent corner of palace III, Hyksos xvth dynasty, at 1021. The base of the tower is about 995, and the main wall of palace III is based at 990. It corresponds therefore with palace III, which is twenty-two feet west of it. A view of the tower, with a survey pole leaning against it, is in pl. xliii, 1.

28. On removing the loose stones which filled the chamber, there was found on the rough stone floor the group of gold armlets and the objects above them on pl. i ; for detail, see pl. ii. There were not any bones or pottery placed with the jewellery. Gold alone was in the chamber. The tower was, then, a cenotaph, not a tomb. When some queen of the city had died, it may have been thought dangerous to place so much gold far out of sight in the cemetery; so the real burial and its offerings of meat and drink with pottery, was in the cemetery, while a cenotaph in front of the palace was both a memorial and a safe deposit for the jewellery.

29. The gold armlets are in two groups of five, each group being numbered from 1 to 11111 by cuts near one end, see pl. ii. (4 J) *. Around each end were fine incised lines, between four and seven in number ; also slight vandyke lines below. The terminal armlets, 1, 2, 9, 10 are rounded on the terminal surface, but flattened where touching the next, see section. All the medial armlets 3 to 8 are flattened on both sides, so as to lie close together. This flattening is entirely original in the making, and not due to wear, as the weight of the terminals averages 692 grains and of the medials 696 grains, though the latter have twice the wear. The specific gravity is 17·2, and therefore probably with 10 per cent. of alloy.

The large earrings above (1 J) have a bar of greyish blue lazuli, tipped at the ends and hooped with gold. The weight of the ring, without the bar, is 291.0 and 291.4 grains. These and the armlets are on the Egyptian qedet unit of weight, and of the same fineness. The size of the bars implies the piercing of wide holes in the ear, and Akhenaten, influenced by Syrian customs, had similar piercings.

* Objects marked J have been chosen for the Jerusalem Museum.

The small ribbed earrings (1 J), are certainly of Asiatic style ; they weigh 57·4 and 58·2 grs. The two toggle-pins (J) weigh 172·3 and 89·1 grs. All of these are on the khoirine unit of North Syria (see list of weights, pl. lviii).

30. The regions where toggle-pins are found give some evidence of the movement of the peoples who brought them to Palestine. Not only do they appear in Mesopotamia, but also in the Caucasus ; a valuable paper in *Eurasia Septentrionalis* vii., 113–182, by Franz Hančar, describes the sites of toggle-pins. They are in the valley of the river Kur, on the eastern slopes facing the Caspian, but none on the slope to the Black Sea. They have both rings and spirals as ornaments, like those of the Hyksos. The inference is that they were used by a people on the west of the Caspian, or in Mesopotamia. These people may well have been those whom we know as North Syrians, of the viith and viiith dynasties in Egypt. Confirming this, toggle-pins of gold are found at MV 983 level, and tomb 1406 at the same level. There were also four of copper in the tombs 1409 and 1410 which are before the xiith dynasty, and down to palace I level at PL 925 (pl. xviii, 202–6). They have not been found in the xiith dynasty, so they may have died out then, and been reintroduced by the Hyksos from the same region.

31. In this group of jewellery was a scaraboid (J) of grey lazuli in a gold mount, but without a hoop (viii, 120). On it is engraved a seated winged dog, and two scorpions in the field. There was also a haematite scarab (J) in a small massive gold ring. The engraving is a figure of the child Horus, with *onkh* before him, and a papyrus plant behind (viii, 121). Some plain pieces of thick sheet gold, perhaps dowels, were also found (J).

The deposit represented the contents of a jewel case, and all the objects were for personal adornment. There was a spacer-bead of gold (I, 1) for a necklace of eight strings of gold beads, but no such beads were found though all the earth was carefully sifted. Also there was a small gold ring from some larger ornament. These must have been the odds and ends of the jewel box. The valuables of a great personage were thus strangely preserved during four thousand years.

32. Pl. III, *Gold work*. 11A to 11H, see pls. iii, iv : 12 ivory. Expiatory deposit. This group belonged to a man, the purgation of whose crime resembled that of Achan (*Josh.* vii, 24). In a pit on the plain west of the city, no. 1504 on plan, pl. l, there was an immense quantity of sooty black ash, the remains of burnt garments. Amid this was goldwork, most carefully destroyed ; the bracelets with serpent's head terminals (iii A) were cut into scraps, the little eyes still gleaming on the severed heads ; the bright plating of gold was stripped from objects and torn into the smallest fragments ; gold-plated studs and nails (iii E, H) were all loose from some woodwork which had been burnt. One ring with leaf terminals (iii B) yet remained, and the hoop (iii C) from which a scarab was broken. All the rest of the gold was melted into lumps and globules. Silver was also mostly melted, and only a few beads remained, as iii F, G, and a ring iii D. The ivory draughtsman (iii, 12) is one of those which endured, partly calcined. Copper was mostly broken up, only two pieces remained in shape, xix, 293, 294 ; the use of them is unknown.

Of stone work there are two basalt tripod stands, xxiii, 46, 47. These had been broken to pieces on the spot, as not a single fragment was missing ; 47 is the finest example of basalt work, with a central pillar, bearing a six-lobed capital (see pl. iv). A large alabaster jar, xxiii, 48, with wide brim, was smashed and burnt ; a smaller one like this was in a Hyksos deposit in Egypt (*Sedment II*, xli, 2). A slate dish (45) was similarly broken up and burnt. A piece of a pottery jar, like xxxi, 38 o⁷, was also found burnt. The level of this jar in the Tell shows that it is of the xiith dynasty, or immediately after. Many teeth of horses and chips of burnt bones were also found.

Here there was a complete destruction of property, with gold and silver, consigned to expiate a great crime, and purge the community from a curse—a very close parallel to the case of Achan. This proves that this mode of communal purgation was a custom of Canaan a thousand years before the Israelite tragedy took place.

33. III, 13. The gold toggle-pin found on body 1165 lay with a scarab of Apepa I and five others, vii, 75–80. The top is split and turned over to retain a ring, which was probably placed to secure a bead of perishable material (glass ?). This is the best dated pin. No. 14 was found with a gold frontlet band, 42, and an alabaster vase, xxii, 7, in a burial beneath the corner of the room MU, below the Hyksos wall. 15 is a gold toggle found in the chamber MV 983, the same level as the previous. 16 is a silver toggle probably late in the xvith

dynasty. 17 to 19 are of the earlier part of the xviiith dynasty, 20, 21 are of the xixth.

22. The crescent or horns amulet with small gold pendants (viii, 117–9) in tomb 1080, was found with the gold ring, vii, 46, of about the mid xviiith dynasty. Another, of 1095, was with scarabs of Amenhetep III, vii. 52–3. The latest form, fig. 23, is clumsily elaborate, and belongs to the xixth dynasty.

34. Torque earrings. Fig. 24 is one of a pair of gold earrings (i J) found with the string of carnelian and gold beads and pendants, at the base of pl. i, tomb 1073. From that tomb there are three scarabs, vii, 39–41, of the age of Tahutmes III, a rough scarab in gold setting, iii, 36, and an empty setting 38, probably of a glass scarab decomposed. The fabric of this twisted earring is that of some Irish earrings (see E.C.R. ARMSTRONG, *Catalogue of Irish Gold Ornaments*, p. 87, xviii, 415–7). Two strips of gold are folded along the whole length at right angles >, and soldered together >< ; this gives a rod with four flanges. Lengths of this are swaged at the ends into a thin rod, and the whole is then coiled into a ring. Such a fabric is found in Britain and in France, doubtless exported from Ireland, which produced most of the western gold. One ring of such fabric was found at Troy (*Ilios*, fig. 593). Four such rings come from Enkomi, Cyprus, (Brit. Mus.) accompanied by about twenty stouter rings, probably made in Cyprus. The distinction is that the Irish examples are so thin that the flanges distort sideways when coiled ; the Cypriote are made stouter so that the gold can flow under tension without distortion, like a solid screw. The examples at Gaza are of the Irish quality, and extend the area of trade connection to the farthest corner of the Mediterranean.

Such a connection at 1450 B.C. is what might be expected, since we know of the transfer to Ireland of lotus and of spiral patterns which were extinct in the Mediterranean by 1200 B.C. (*Decorative Patterns*, p. 9). It is in accord with the strong tradition of such migration, and it is also substantiated by Sir Arthur Keith's conclusion that skulls show a steady infusion of people from the Mediterranean as well as from the Rhine.

35. III, 25 was with the earring 17. 26 is of dyn. xviii. 27 is a Hat-hor pendant of dyn. xviii found with the larger dagger, xiv, 77 ; arrow heads, xvi, 136–7, xvii, 154–7, 160 ; bangle 172 and the group xxiv, 26–31. It is of impressed gold foil attached to a foil back. The silver pendant earring, 28, was with the figure and rosettes, vii, 174, 184, also bronze earrings xvii, 178, and beads xxv, 100–107. The silver crescent pendant, 29, was with a Hyksos scarab vii, 107, a silver disc 41, two toggles xviii, 218–9, and an amethyst scarab in bronze ring, 246.

Figs. 30–33, group 1037, are dated to Amenhetep II, scarab 19, with a silver ram viii, 176, many arrow heads, and five alabasters, 14, 18, 21, 30, 33.

34, A string of gold and carnelian beads was with two scarabs of dyn. xviii (vii, 72–3), a silver ring with figure of Ptah (iii, 44), and alabaster vases xxii, 22, 27, 31. The gold beads were made by pressing in a cup mould, and then uniting the two cups around the edges. 35, lotus pendant, was with the gold earring 24, pl. i. figs. 36, 38, see 24. 39 is of late xviiith dynasty.

36. Pls. X–XIII have been described in Chapter II. Fig. 68 is of a different fabric from the other daggers, with two incised lines along the axis; also it is corroded and this suggests that it is alloyed. It cannot be analysed as it was kept at Jerusalem. There was no pottery with it, but the tomb and burial were like those of the copper daggers.

XIV. 69 is probably a lance-head; by the level, it is of the xiith dynasty. Fig. 70 was with pottery of dyn. xvi; the tang and hole for pegging it, and the round end, differ entirely from any others here.

71 has raised veins on the face, and side clutches to the handle. It was set in a wooden handle covered with sheet bronze, and having a white stone ball pommel. The wood had entirely decayed, and the bronze was crushed flat. With this were two spear-heads, 72, and a narrow axe of Mesopotamian type (all J). The only pottery with it was a large jar of oval outline, 43 D8; this is most like 43 E7, which is from 1408 in the court-yard, and therefore of dyn. x–xi. The axe 73 is known in the xiith dynasty.

The other example of a veined dagger, 74, had also a narrow spear-head, 75, with it. It was in one of the courtyard tombs, associated with the usual pottery of that group, and there is no reason for its not being of the xth–xith dynasties, like the rest of that cemetery. Thus both the veined daggers are of one period.

76. This long dagger with a mid-rib is of about xviiith dynasty, but the arrow-heads and pottery with it do not fix the date. 77 is of the same type,

but with a smooth blade; for the group, see iii, 27, sect. 35.

37. XV, 78. Tubular cover for a staff, from a plain burial, no pottery. 79–80. Tubular cover for handle, with axe, also arrow-heads 114–6, and alabaster kohl-pot xxii, 19; early in dyn. xviii.

81. Razor of usual form, with knife xix, 267, and pin xviii, 237; dyn. xviii.

82. Mirror with square handle, so probably Syrian, the Egyptian being triangular; with alabaster xxiii, 29, mid dyn. xviii. 83. Mirror with bronze dish xxiii, 41, and arrow-heads, see last group in pl. xxi; all of dyn. xviii. 84, Mirror from fosse tomb, dyn. xix. Armlets, 85 of x–xi. 86 of xxii, with the four heavy anklets 88, and a great quantity of bead necklaces, also Cypriote vases. 87, fragment of bracelet, Hyksos. 89, four heavy anklets from 1067 of same age as 88. These anklets are probably intended to be two *debens* in weight in accord with the meaning of the word; the original weight of the remitted examples is 88, 2740 and 2620 grs., 89, 2860 and 2680; those at Jerusalem have not been cleaned.

90. A plain disc of bronze. The wire bangles are common; for the groups, see the registers, lvi–lix.

38. XVI, XVII. A great quantity of copper arrow-heads were found, from half-a-dozen to a score in a single grave. They are of mid and late Hyksos, and of dyn. xviii. The few thicker lance-heads are 98–101. The levelled arrow-heads from the city are 103–127; from graves 129–160, approximately in historic order as far as can be gathered. The metal is always flexible, and not deeply corroded, and it cleans perfectly to bright metal, so it is nearly pure copper. They were cast with a duct at the tip. Sometimes along with these are bullet arrows 161–168 for fowling, as from the tomb of Tutankhamen. This makes it probable that the large arrow-heads were for hunting rather than for war. The smaller bangles and finger rings are entered in the registers, pls. lvi–lix.

39. Pl. XVIII. Toggle-pins. These are first found in the 1400 cemetery of the palace courtyard, certainly before the xiith dynasty, and to be classed as xth–xith dynasties. These pins here prove that the toggle was brought in before the Hyksos came; and probably by the people of the viith dynasty—the first palace, see sect. 26. Those from the cemetery, 209–219, are mostly of dyn. xviii. In gold work there is a fine one, 18, dated to Apepa I. So it appears that the use of the toggle extended through the Hyksos age into the xviiith dynasty. Of the latter age is a gold one from Gurob (*Objects of Daily Use*, p. 6 ; ii. 13).

Needles and hair-pins, 220–240, are mostly of late period. 234 has a bone head attached ; it is dated to Amenhetep II. The kohl sticks squared in the middle to give a hold, 253–258, are only known of Roman age, and perhaps Arab. The low levels of these must be due to the denudation of the eastern side of the courtyard. The toilet spoons 259–263 are also later.

40. XIX. A chisel, 264, with a half-socket for the handle, is like the daggers in *Beth-pelet* I, xi, 82, *Gaza* I, xix, 41. The double-edged knife, 267, is of a form which was usual in dyn. xviii. The thick brand, 272, is of a type usual in Egypt in dyns. xviii–xix (*T.W.* lxxi, 49) ; the goose here was probably supplemented by a disc for Ra, to mark the royal title " Son of the Sun " on the animal.

274 is in imitation of a Chinese mirror, due to mediaeval Arab trade. The silver tweezer, 284, was found in a pit, so is probably Arab.

293, 294 are pieces of bronze work, found burnt in the accursed deposit, 1504 (sect. 32). The small measure of bronze, fig. 300, found with the dagger, fig. 76, we had no means of gauging before it passed to the Jerusalem Museum.

41. XX. *Iron work.* 303, this spear-head was discovered at the late Hyksos level, just in front of the palace ; as that ground was denuded to this level, it may belong to the early Iron Age. The iron mace-head, 305, was in a tomb, 1011, of early Iron Age. It is rusted all through, and the outline here is restored to original form by deduction from the weight.

CHAPTER VI
SCARABS

42. VII. SCARABS from cemetery. These are placed here in order of the tomb numbers, for convenience of reference in groups. The unusual ones are the following. 15 seal with dog and oryx, dyn. xviii. 32 bronze ring, reading *Amen the Great*, xviii. 42, 43 seals found in the Solomonic burial, 1074, with Cypriote vases, large anklets, and many strings of beads (xxv, 76–92), see plan liii ; 42 is of the oriental drill work, 43 is finely cut on sard, like early Greek gems. 59 has with it a silver setting and loop for suspension. 64, 65 were with the silver Hathor ring, iii. 43. 72, 73 were

with a string of gold and carnelian beads (1147). 74 bears a fine figure of a prince of the Hyksos age (1163). The group 75–80 is dated by 77, of Apepa I, the only dated Hyksos material in this season ; with these, placed on the breast, was the fine gold toggle-pin, iii, 13. The great tomb, 1166, contained many scarabs, 81 to 101, on the numerous burials, see pl. liii ; it was a family tomb, of the xviiith dynasty to Rameses II. Nos. 103 to 106 were on the courtyard burials, 1406–1410, probably of X–XIth dynasty.

43. VIII. 111–118 scarabs from known levels. 111–112 of dyn. xviii have been dropped to a lower level by denudation ; others are at their correct levels. 116 is an impress with a very rare figure of a giraffe, connected with those figured at Deir el Bahri by Hatshepsut. 117 is a sherd of pale brown hard pottery, stamped with the names of Hatshepsut and Tehutmes III, during their brief co-regency about 1481 B.C. The scarabs of hard stone, 120, 121, belong to the' cenotaph deposit, see sect. 31.

122 to 135 were picked up loose on the surface of the cemetery, 1000, and have no connections. 123 is a copy of a scarab of Amenemhat III. 124 seems to have a figure in tall boots, connected perhaps with the Hittite large boots.

143–168 have been picked up about the site. 143 has the rare name of Ra-ne-maot, probably the 48th of the xiiith dyn., Sebekhetep IX. 164 is of a curious fabric of relief in faience, glazed. 167 belongs to the first year of Ramessu II, by the form of the *user*.

Among the small objects and pendants there is a bronze seated figure, 173, apparently a deity, with pointed cap and outspread wings, found with scarab 22 and pottery, tomb 1049, xxii ? Also from the group 1037 the silver sheep 176, scarab 19 of Amenhetep II, and fine alabasters xxii, 14, 18, 21, 30, 33.

CHAPTER VII
STONE WORK

44. PL. XXII. 1. IN the Copper Age cemetery were found three natural lumps of limestone, perforated ; similar lumps were seen at Gerar. The perforation is conical, from each side (see the section), and could not retain a handle. Similar stones are used by the Bedawy to-day, for weighting down tents in a wind, by throwing a rope over the tent with a stone at each end. It is possible that tents were thus secured in the Copper Age. No habitations of that period have yet been found at Gaza, and tents may have been in use.

2 to 6. Basalt and trachyte bowls. Their fabrication begins in the south with the people from the Jordan valley, in the middle Neolithic, and continued till late times. The finest examples known are the two table stands, 46–47, see sect. 32.

7. Alabaster found with gold frontlet and toggle-pin, with a burial under the foundation of the first Hyksos palace.

9. Only one mace-head was found ; it was of the age of the first palace.

10–13. These small spindle-whorls are indications of delicate spinning in Hyksos times. 14 was with the silver sheep, see sect. 43. 16 with finger ring 43. 17 with broken oval steatite vase, 25, and copper bangle 172. 19 with the bronze axe, xv, 79–80, and arrow-heads, early xviii. 22 in tomb 1147 with 27, 31 and bronze ; 72–3, scarabs of xviii ; silver ring 44, and beads of cupped gold 34.

23 is well wrought in black serpentine, early xviii. 24 is of Hyksos age. 26 is probably of late xvi ; 27, 28 of xviii.

45. XXIII. 29–34 are all of xviii. 35–40 of Ramessu II. 42, 43 were with pottery 51 P8, probably late Hyksos. 44 is perhaps part of an alabaster gaming board.

45–48 stone vessels, broken up in the " Achan " deposit, 1504, see sect. 32, pl. iv.

49. Sard finger-ring from 1166 tomb, Ramessu II.

50. Flints of a sickle, found in position, though the wood had decayed ; with painted jar 37 J2'.

CHAPTER VIII

BONE, BEADS AND GLASS

46. XXIV. BONE. Two early pieces of engraved bone were found, fig. 1 on the basal marl, and 2 to 7 in a chamber of palace I, at 10 ins. over the stone basing. Thus both are before the xiith dynasty. 3 represents a captive, with a Syrian robe, but a wig head-dress like an Egyptian. It may represent an Egyptian of rank, prisoner of the Syrian viith dynasty, granted a Syrian robe for the climate.

8–11, 20, bone with ring pattern ; these look like Arabic strays on the denuded surface.

16 rod of bone, xii dyn. 17, 18, 33 are of xix. 19 was with the Solomonic group, 1074, see sect. 42.

26–31 are from a large group, tomb 1514, with gold Hathor head, 27, and large dagger 77.

47. XXV. Beads are arranged by their level in the town, to show their period ; from the cemetery the arrangement is by tomb number. Corresponding objects are in the registers, lvi to lix.

48. XXVI. Glass and paste. 136 is a restoration from fragments of glazed quadruple kohl-tubes, of the Hyksos age : the tube form was therefore used in Syria before it entered Egypt under Tahutmes III. 137, paste vase decomposed by damp, late Hyksos. 138, blue paste cup of xxiind dynasty.

139–141, glass vases much decomposed by damp, all of dyn. xviii.

142 is the form of glazed beads found with early scarabs in the X–XIth dyn. cemetery, 1406.

143–4 were with a scarab of Amenhetep II, in a large group, see register lvi. Plan of the palaces superposed, see sects. 2 to 5.

CHAPTER IX

THE FOREIGN POTTERY

49. Pls. XXXVIII–XLI. MUCH more of the painted pottery from foreign sources was found, in continuation of the varieties published in *Gaza* I, xxviii–xxxiv. The definite palace levels and dates being known, it was possible to fix the ages of pottery found in that connection. Every piece of distinctive pottery from the palaces and courtyard was levelled and the place of it marked on it ; thus we are in a position to study the whole effectively. Mr. O'Brien with, later, Mrs. Warren Hastings were most careful in preserving this record.

The first question is about the uniformity of level of any period, and the risk of disturbance. From the beginning of the work, we found that the floors of the upper buildings did not vary more than an inch or two. The most decisive test, over the whole area and at all levels, was from the fine Anatolian decoration being superseded by the coarse Cypriote imitation of it. There were more than three hundred fragments of these wares, so casual variation was immaterial. If from any cause there were irregular levels, we should find that the transition from the fine to the coarse painting was widely spread. On the contrary, the beginning of the Cypriote series is only 17 ins. below the end of the fine Anatolian, and the coarse Anatolian lasted but little later. Some period of mixture must have occurred during the fading out of imports of fine ware, and the establishing of the Cypriote imitation. But 17 ins. for the whole period of admixture, leaves no room for more than a foot depth of accidental confusion. There are a few exceptional cases, far from the continuous series, due to Arab mixture by digging grain-pits, and throwing out early material at a higher level; but on pl. xxxvii. the curves of distribution of the two styles make it evident where the continuous series begins and ends, and what are the sporadic single examples due to disturbance.

In this diagram, xxxvii, the height of the curves shows the number of examples found in each 10 ins. of level. The vertical lines divide each 20 ins. of level. The Anatolian is a broken curve, and the Cypriote is the full line. The apparent extent of overlap is rather diffused owing to counting by 10-inch groups, but the individual examples of first and last at the overlap are as stated above. This result agrees with the observation of horizontal bedding in the plans, so that the level seems fixed as probably significant to the nearest foot, or century, of the history.

The sources of most of the painted pottery are yet unknown. None of the students of the Nearer East have identified the locality of such wares, partly owing to the lack of excavation north of Palestine, partly owing to later material hiding the remains earlier than 2000 B.C.

50. XLII. The range of each kind of decoration is marked on this diagram; each distinct class of ornament has a line; each 10 ins. of level has a column, with the level in inches above sea marked at the top. Each specimen found is entered in place, by the two letters of the chamber or area where found, referring to pl. xlviii. The broad distinctions of the five palaces are shown by thick vertical lines at the general separation.

It will be seen how the Arab digging of pits has thrown up sporadic examples. For instance, the Vandyke is mostly at 980–9, while two bits appear at 1050 and 1070; the plaited band is found continuously from 930–1030, and then two sporadic pieces at 1060, 1070; the 'Union Jack' pattern is from 930 to 1010, and then one stray at 1100. This table is not to be used blindly, but with due regard to the small proportion of scattered material, which we see must have resulted from the numerous grain-pits of Arab settlers. It is the continuity in the levels of a type which is the decisive evidence.

The broad result is that almost all the forms of

decoration started in the first palace period, and lasted through the time of the second palace, or xiith dynasty. The decline is seen as soon as the Hyksos were well established, at about 1030 level. Whether this change was due to a general decline of civilisation about 2100 B.C., or due to broken trade routes cutting off the distant supply, may be traceable in future. Certainly the fine quality of pottery and painted design in fig. 11, at 1013 level, does not look like a decline in work.

The value of the Gaza site is not only for its own history. It was a main gathering ground for fine work from elsewhere, imported for the palace of the greatest ruler in South Syria; these foreign works are here dated by a long succession of palaces, identified with the known history of Egypt, and providing regular levels of the site. Here we can sample and put in historic position the arts of which we have not yet found the sources; and our dating here will serve to clear up the future discoveries in the Eastern Mediterranean.

51. XXXVIII–XL. These plates are classified by the nature of the objects represented, quadrupeds, birds, fish, cross, zigzag, lily, and stitch patterns. Vertical shading is for red. It is useless to describe what is obvious on the plates, but some details need attention.

Figs. 1 and 11 are akin, by the good drawing and a peculiarly brilliant red colour; they were found at opposite ends of the site, but at the same level (compare *Gaza* I, xxviii, 5). At the right end of 11 is part of a form like that of 12. 3 is the latest and worst quadruped figure. 15 shows a little Egyptian influence. 14 is a horn in the round, probably from a head of Hathor.

18 is almost the earliest fish figure. 20, 21, 22, 25 are " Maltese " crosses, also found last year, *G.* I, xxx, 23–26; these belong to the time of the viiith to xiith dynasties.

24, 25 are parts of a large vase found in the cemetery, tomb 1146. They were completely encrusted with lime, and it was only when cleaned in London that they were found to be coloured; this is a history like that of no. 5 last year.

26, 27 are thin bowls of polished white face with chocolate brown pattern; only small pieces of these were found, 26 lay at 950 and 955 level, 27 at 958 and 985. Another piece of the same ware is 28, found at 990 between the bones of a Hyksos skeleton. The chocolate and white pottery is the finest fabric, with a hard body as white as porcelain in the best examples, and a bright white face well polished. A fine specimen is the bowl iv, 1, which was found loose in the cemetery (J). Among the examples of this fabric last year (G. I, xxxii), no. 59 has the running spiral degraded from the form in the xiith dynasty and also found at Butmír in Bosnia.

33 shows how pieces were thrown up in pit digging ; the top part was at 1017, close to other examples, but the bottom piece which joins it was at 1090, six feet higher : date early in dyn. xv.

34, 35, this metopic design with red or black diagonals is usually on thin fine bowls, with brilliant red.

39, 40, are of strange matt-faced soft ware. The lily with withered spathe is known on a jasper scarab of the xiith dynasty, the age of 39 here. The running spiral on 40, with buds in the angles, is found in the xiith dynasty. There is, then, no reason to doubt these being of palaces II and III, in accord with the levels.

XLI, see pls. iv, v. The succession of Anatolian and Cypriote bowls has been already described, as evidence for the level stratification of the site, sect. 49. Fig. 42 is a strange style, unique in this place. 43, a duck head on a bowl. 44, one of six legs of pottery dolls ; tomb 1080 xviii dynasty, probably Aegean. Figs. 45 and onward are Arabic.

52. Of the sources of the painted pottery not much can yet be determined. The styles are mostly unknown in origin, and the value of the specimens here lies in the dating which can be assigned by the levels, and will serve to date their occurrence elsewhere. In these few notes I have used Prof. J. L. Myres' paper on the *Early pot-fabrics of Asia Minor*, *J. Anthrop Inst.* xxxiii, 367–398, and Genouillac, *Céramique Cappadocienne.*

Much of what is here has been already found in Cyprus ; the Anatolian and Cypriote bowls, the wheel in a spiral (*Gaza* I, xxx, 31–3), the birds no. 11 (xxxviii), the fluted vase type 59 A, the thin brown with relief bands 89 F, brown with white lines, the red on black bowls 10 U, and the black incised 60 M, are all in the British Museum. The brown ware is doubtless of Cypriote origin ; the animal paintings come from some other source, for the massive and hard pottery is from the mainland.

The best indication of origin is the colouring. The vivid red differs from any native to Palestine or Cyprus, and agrees with the red " better than that of any other country " from Cappadocia (Strabo XII, ii, 10). The same paragraph describes the

" ivory white " pottery of the meerschaum clay near Kaisariyeh which agrees with the frequent class of white pottery, often with chocolate lines, 26–29 here, and *G.* I, 55–62. This Cappadocian connection agrees (Gen., *C.C.*, pls. 25, 39) with the patterns of checkers, *G.* I, 56, and pieces this year : also with the vandykes, Gen., *C.C.* I, 9, the diagonal squares divided, 37 here and at Boghaz-koi, *G., C.C.* I., and the hour-glass type as Gen., *C.C.* pl. 52.

The plaited pattern, 19, 22 here, is at Ur and Kouyunjik, also common in the West, Crete to Britain. The ' Union Jack ' pattern and wheel are not yet placed to any site ; the Maltese cross is rare in Assyria, and in early Crete (M.M. 1), though common in late times in the Mediterranean. So the decoration that can be identified, and the colouring, agree on the Cappadocian connection, while the other styles are yet to seek.

The early dating of much of this pottery is surprising. On the diagram xiii, most of the styles begin about the viiith dynasty, and no good ware survives the xvth. Broadly, it is 3000 to 2000 B.C. that was the great age of decoration. The Cypriote wares go back in several styles to the viith dynasty, 3100 B.C.

CHAPTER X
NOTES ON PLATES

53. XLIII. THE views here have been noted in connection with the different palaces. Fig. 1 shows the method of placing the slabs and blocks of sandstone for the walls of the first palace. Behind it at a higher level is the cenotaph of the xvth dynasty. On the nearest corner of that is a large displaced block of sandstone, the seat of a privy, but not fitting to the marks on the bathroom floors of either palace I or II. 2 is a chamber in palace III, lined with white plaster, in many successive coats. On the long wall face is seen the mark about 5 ft. up, where the later walling extended before we cut it away. 3 shows the succession of alterations, walls 1, 2 before the xiith dyn., 3, 4, of the xiith, 5 of the xvth, 6, 7, alterations by the xvith. The pile in the corner of 5–6 is filling of earth left in place for a step in our excavation.

XLIV. 1 is the white plastered bathroom of palace I. It was reached by two steps, at the right hand, in which was set the water-jar that is outlined on pl. xlv. From this there runs to the left the stone basing of the wall, of which a part of the brickwork remains.

2 is the revetment of the city bank, and the stone road along the foot of it. In 3 the only drum of a stone column appears, built over by palace II. 4 is the white-plastered bathroom of palace II; the walls have been systematically removed for bricks to build palace III. 5 is a bath with steps covered with white stucco, in the cemetery ground north-east of the palace. It must be older than the earliest buildings there, as the wall ran over it; yet later than burial 1409, which it partly overlies, see pl. xlviii. 6 is the cenotaph in which the Hyksos jewellery was deposited.

54. XLV. The plan of palace I of the viith dynasty is described in sects. 10, 11, 12. It was contemporary with the great fosse, of which the section is here; that supplied the stone for the palace. The jar is that at the palace bathroom, and is therefore of the vith or viith dynasty, and much older than any other such jar at Byblos, or later in the Hyksos age. At the base of the plate is the detailed plan and section of the large sunken way, on the north-east of the cemetery in li, lii. The purpose of this trench is obscure; it does not lead to any tomb or other work, it rises abruptly at one end, it does not cut across any exposed ridge of land. For the dromos to a tomb, if unfinished, it would be far too long.

XLVI. Here the previous plan is outlined, and this shows how completely it was ignored by the builders of palace II in the xiith dynasty. As there are two or three feet of washed-down earth between the stone and the later building, the people of the xiith dynasty would have seen only mouldering stumps of the brick walls, and not know of the great stone basing. The door sill of stone marks OF as the entrance hall; OG was the main hall, 21 × 22 ft., which probably had a central pillar to carry roof beams. OH being the bathroom, the chambers behind that would be bedrooms, and the long hall 33 × 8 ft. was the private store-room. The corner chamber MV has been entirely removed by the Hyksos in their appropriation of brick. The drain from the bathroom was hidden beneath the courtyard of that period. It was merely a soak-away.

In the courtyard there was a cemetery which must be before the xiith dynasty palace II; this is indicated by the level, and also the pottery in it is unlike any of the Hyksos age, and a form of pan

is found with pottery of the Copper Age, see base of pl. xxxvi. All the forms here are characteristically early, see Register lviii. The tombs are sunk in the marl, and the largest were chambers cut entirely in the rock, such as 1417, with a slain donkey buried high up over the entrance.

XLVII. The interior of 1417 is shown in xlvii, 1, and the veined dagger in xiv, 74. The attitude is plainly that of death, and not owing to the decomposition of an orderly laid body; in particular, the spread of the right arm could not occur by any falling apart. As a contrast, see the precise burial of 1413 next to it. The cutting across the great fosse gives some idea of the depth of it; the slope at the back is that up the city bank. At the side of the lowest workman is the square shaft down to a large tomb of the xixth dynasty, 1166, planned in liii. The section of the fosse is on xlv.

XLVIII. The remainder of the cemetery is placed later, on pl. xlviii, as the relation to the walls above it is important. Obviously tombs 1407 and 1409 must have preceded the walls, but those walls are based only twenty inches above the marl. They are of the same level as the Hyksos palace III in that plate; as the tombs cannot be of the xiith dynasty when palace II was important, they must precede that. In 1403 is a brick sarcophagus; the entry was to the west, blocked by stones. Similarly in 1404 the entry was by 1406, blocked by bricks; and in 1407 the entry was on the west, blocked by stones. The types of pottery in the northern tombs up to 1409 are practically the same as in the southern 1410 and on, see lviii.

55. The palace III had massive walls, over eight feet thick in front; it had few chambers and no bathroom. The equally massive building to the north has no obvious meaning. A large solid block of brickwork to the south of it looks like the base of a tower. It seems to have been a residence, as it has cesspits, ML, and a drain through the wall. The revetment is entered on plan xlviii, to show how it was ruined and disregarded when building these walls across it, only four inches above the stones. The cenotaph, 1450, in the courtyard has been described, in discussing the jewellery found in it, sect. 27. The letters given to areas, for marking the place of pottery found here, are all entered on this plan, as it is nearly related to the courtyard; the open outline of palace II is shown.

The shaded parts of palace chambers show where the walls were thickened to resist the collapse of the back wall. The top of the thickening was the floor of the next occupation.

XLIX. Palace IV of the later Hyksos, xvith dynasty, was partly identical with the walls of III, with floors raised 52 inches. At the north end of the northern building some irregular brick chambers, NA . . ., were added, over a mass of sandstone grit. The great bank of the city wall was continually extended outward, and the western chambers MF, MG, rest on this new ground.

Palace V of the xviiith dynasty is distinguished by its being carried still further west ; but as it is on the top it has been heavily denuded, so that there is only fifteen inches' height left of it, tapering off to nothing on the north.

Of Arab times there were traces of irregular lines of rough stones in a few parts, not enough to give any connected idea of a building. Such was all that remained of the camp of Malik al Kamil in A.D. 1227 ; or of the Mamluk beacon station which ended the chain of signals from the Euphrates ; hence to Cairo the link was by pigeon post. Mr. C. H. Johns, who informs me of this, also states that the Arab glazed wares here resemble those from 'Atlit, or more nearly from 'Ajlun, which were both occupied by the Ayyubids, and Mamluks, xiiith to xvth centuries A.D. To this period therefore must be assigned the design pottery, pl. xli.

L. The founding of the later Hyksos palace IV was signalised by digging a pit in the walls of palace III (xlviii). In this pit a horse was thrown after removal of the shoulders for eating, and the left thigh. On the new ground level, about 1060, there were the scattered bones of two other horses which had been eaten. Such a sacrifice would be impossible to Egyptians, and stamps this as the Hyksos level. Two and a half feet higher is found the pottery of Tehutmes III and Hatshepsut (viii).

Another field of bones was some way beyond the outer end of the long tunnel. In this spread, the remarkable burial of severed limbs is unexplained. There is a whole human arm, but no scapula ; a whole leg and a piece of hip, but no more ; many skulls, but no vertebrae. Of animals there are various limbs and skulls of ass, gazelle, horse, and ox. Near by, a smaller patch of broken bones and pottery contained sherds of fine Anatolian, but no Cypriote bowls. This throws the date back to the 980 level of the Tell, the middle of the xiith dynasty or earlier.

CHAPTER XI

THE CEMETERIES

56. LI. On the right hand of this plate is marked a " deep pit." Above this pit were the burials just named. It was entirely filled up by washed-in earth before the limb burials took place, as they were over the pit. As the pit is probably due to the great excavators of the fosse, vi–viith dynasty, the filling up of it is due to the age of denudation which succeeded that, and washed about eight feet off the surface of the ground. Thus the limb burial is limited to the age just before the Egyptian occupation by the xiith dynasty, as such burial of limbs is entirely un-Egyptian. In all this we have a curiously close fitting of evidences which leaves only a century or two of uncertainty, though solely by inference from material facts.

The tunnel found last year, and cleared out through 500 ft., was entirely washed away at the end nearest to the city gate. This year we found at a lower level another tunnel, which was probably the substitute when the upper one was destroyed. Where this lower tunnel goes we do not yet know ; a small portion of it found last year was then supposed to be the edge of the gangway into the city, but the opposite side has now been found, proving it to be a passage.

The purpose of the three " deep pit " sites, two found last year and one in this year, to the west, is yet quite unexplained. The narrow trenches or channels shown on the plan were for irrigation canals, see lii.

The cemetery to the west, near the corner of the city, was mainly of the xviiith dynasty ; some tombs were of Hyksos age, and others of the xxiind dynasty. The " sunk way " on the north has been already described (sect. 54, base of pl. xlv).

The most notable tomb was no. 1037, pl. liii, described with that plate. Away to the west of the city, about a quarter of a mile distant, was the cemetery of the Copper Age, outlined here in its correct relation to the city. As an inset on this plate there is, on the right, the detailed plan of the position of the tombs, described in sect. 7. For the whole of the cemetery surveys we are particularly indebted to the care of Mr. G. F. Royds, O.B.E., who has most kindly helped us a second year.

57. LII. The cemetery of the xviiith dynasty occupied the higher ground north of the Tell. Not only was this all turned over by us, but also the ground elsewhere around it, as outlined on li.

The tombs vary much in form. Each type is lettered on liii, and the letter is placed in the third column of the register of tombs, lvi to lix. Some burials were made on the ground sloping down into the deep pit : three out of the five so placed were cremation burials.

The long narrow trenches can only be explained as irrigation channels, made before the sand had blown over the surface. To the east of the cemetery is a large well, with stairway leading down, and a central shaft of stone placed later for drawing water by a rope. The top of this is at 811 level. (The written numbers are for levels, the printed numbers for tombs.) To the north a channel runs down to 745 level, where it ends in a sump pit, from which water could be drawn. Another channel runs to the south from 811 to 809 level. A long channel runs to the west from 820 to 801, 789, 775, 764, 751, 734. There another well appears, and would seem to have supplied further on to 767, 763, ending at 751. These continuous falls from the wells seem to prove that water control was the purpose. The long straight channel through the cemetery runs from 904 in the middle, sloping to 763 on south, and to 882 on north. No well was observed at the middle, but as we only sought for burials it may have been passed over.

The sunk ways are of quite a different character, too wide for irrigation supply, which would soak away, and deeper in the middle than at the ends. The levelled section of the largest (xlv) seems quite inexplicable. The shaded rectangles in the north-east corner are some of the many trial pits which we made in search of cemeteries.

On the south of the plan is marked the Great Fosse, cut in the dune sandstone ; it is almost vertical on the outer side, and slopes up at about 35° to the city bank. The section cut across it was near the north-west corner of the city, the highest ground, where it could be cleared above water-level. The section is on xlv. A rock tomb, 1166, was cut, under the xviiith dynasty, in the city slope (see foot of xlv, and liii). A few plain burials were in the ditch.

Scattered burials west of the city are not recorded here, as more will be done in that region. The straight " line of shells " to the south of the cemetery is about two feet wide ; the shells are laid closely together, but there were no tombs found within a hundred feet of the band, though the whole ground was searched. The band was higher on the north side, as if it were a southern boundary of an area.

58. LIII. The types of the tombs are drawn here, from good examples, and lettered CS to SC, for reference in the registers of tombs. No. 1037 was the most considerable tomb, having a stairway, a lining of large stones, and a roof now destroyed. Though anciently robbed, it still contained a few small gold ornaments, a silver ram amulet, three good alabaster vases and two saucers, besides 26 bronze arrow-heads and a scarab of Amenhetep II, with three common pots. So far, no trace has been found of the great tombs due to rulers of the city when independent, but only the cenotaph with jewellery of that age.

The rock tomb 1166 in the side of the fosse contained about a dozen burials. Some were evidently thrust on one side, to the right hand at A, confused and broken. These had a scarab of Tehutmes III and another which might be as early.

The burials at C had scarabs and a jasper ring which might be of the time of Sety I. Those at D, E, had scarabs entirely of Rameses II. The tomb seems, then, to have been cut in the most flourishing age, under Tehutmes, and to have been despoiled, and altered with enlarged chamber under Rameses.

The burial 1074, in a plain trench, was the latest in the cemetery, of the xxist dynasty. It was notable for the great quantity of bead necklaces of carnelian and glass, besides wristlets ; a remarkable scarab of sard with an animal which was like early Aegean work, a haematite seal with figures of horsemen fighting (vii, 42, 43), two heavy anklets on each leg weighing about two *deben* each, and 42 small pottery flasks, many of Cypriote work. This abundance of fine beads reflects again the wealth of the Solomonic age, as at Beth-pelet (*B.* I, 23).

LIV. Selected burials. 1521 is one of the best of the Copper Age tombs, in the north-east of that cemetery, with a large dagger broken across by a fall of the roof, and bones of an animal, but no vase. 1462 is a group of four bodies ; two originals were laid face to face, a child over them, and lastly a large man placed head to foot of the previous ; by the level these were of Hyksos age.

1514 was a rich tomb in the plain to the west (top corner in lii). It contained a gold Hathor amulet (iii. 27), a large dagger (xiv. 77), many copper arrow-heads, a bone kohl-tube, and a dozen forms of pottery. It was evidently re-used, having bones of an earlier burial pushed away beyond the heads.

1406, 1405 are burials of the x–xith dynasties in the courtyard. 1406 had the greatest variety of pottery, ten pieces, and two fine scarabs (103, 104). The entrance was carefully walled across with brickwork.

59. We can now sum up the new position that we gain by this season's work. The most important clue lies in the toggle-pins. These are known on the coast of the Caspian up as far as the Caucasus, but not on the Black Sea slope. They also appear in Iraq, but are rarely found elsewhere. They were introduced into Palestine by the Hyksos. They also occur in the pre-xiith cemetery of the courtyard of our palaces, and probably belong therefore to the Ist palace. Moreover two daggers with raised lines of veining were found in tombs belonging to the pre-xiith age, and such are found on the Kur river in the Caucasus (*Eurasia Septentrionalis*, vii, 88) but not, apparently, elsewhere. It seems, then, that the people of the palaces I and III came from the same region.

Thus six eastern invasions are known, the conquerors each coming down Syria and subduing Egypt.

The last of these was Saladin the Kurd, with Turkoman troops.

Before him, about 950 B.C. we find evidence in models of box waggons with smooth and spiked wheels, found at Gaza and Gerar, similar to those known from Anau in Turkestan and from Assyria. This movement of people was probably headed by Sheshenq, named after the Persian great god Shushenqu, " He of Susa."

Before that came the Hyksos of palace III, about 2,300 B.C.

Earlier there came the builders of palace I, the North Syrians, who went on into Egypt to found dynasties vii–viii.

Yet before that, there was an eastern migration of the Gerzean people (predynastic Egyptian), bringing lazuli in, and introducing face-veils.

Then, before all the others, there was the Badarian migration, which brought emmer wheat from the Caucasus into Egypt. The place-names of the Caucasus are embedded in the earliest mythology of Egypt (*Ancient Egypt*, 1926, 41 ; 1928, 20). The continual repetitions of invasion from the same region re-inforce the validity of the conclusions. We have here a general view which gives a frame to Asiatic movements over eight or ten thousand years.

The places to which objects have been assigned are marked by initial letters in the Registers, and at top left side in the plates.

A Aberdeen. B Belfast. Bn Bolton. By Batley. E Ethnological, Cambridge. F Fitzwilliam, Cambridge. G Glasgow. H Hull. I Ipswich. J Jerusalem. L London. M Manchester. N Newcastle. O Oxford. Q Reading. R Rochdale. W Wellcome Medical Museum.

Small letters indicate the place of a part of the group.

INDEX

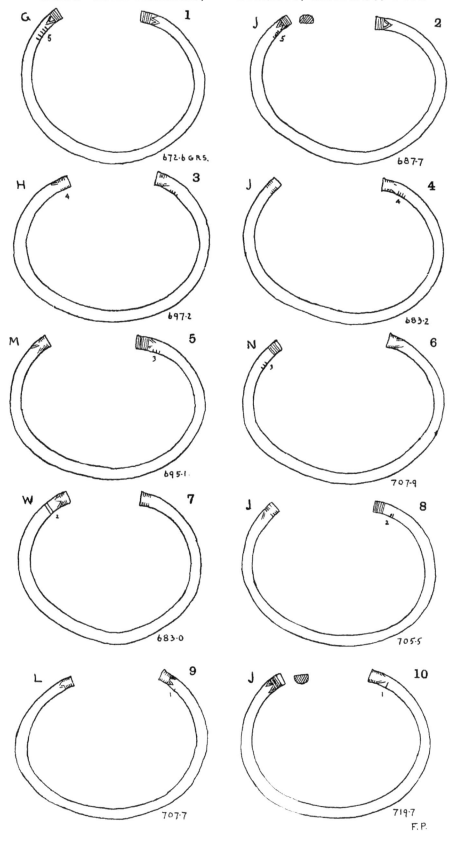

F.P.

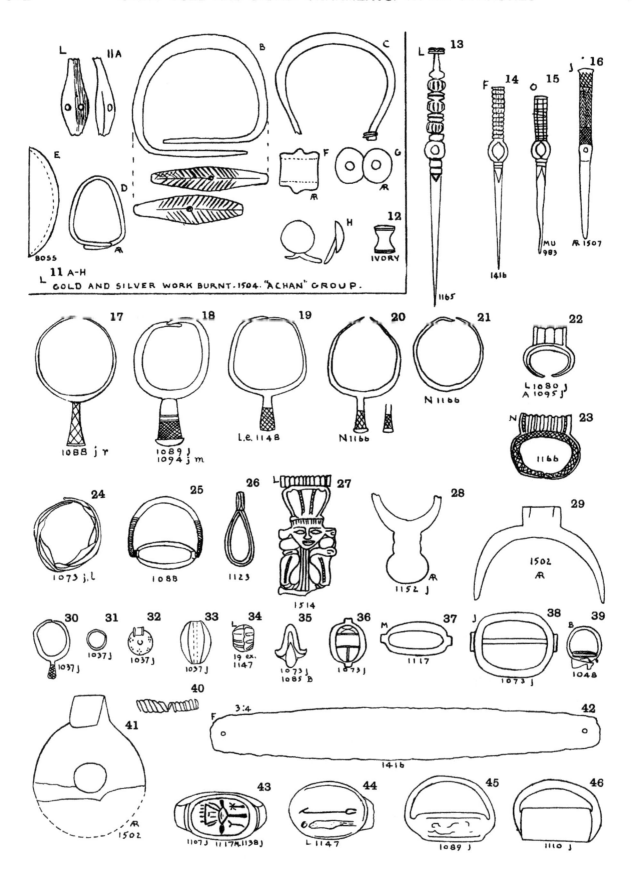

GOLD AND SILVER WORK BURNT.1504. "ACHAN" GROUP.

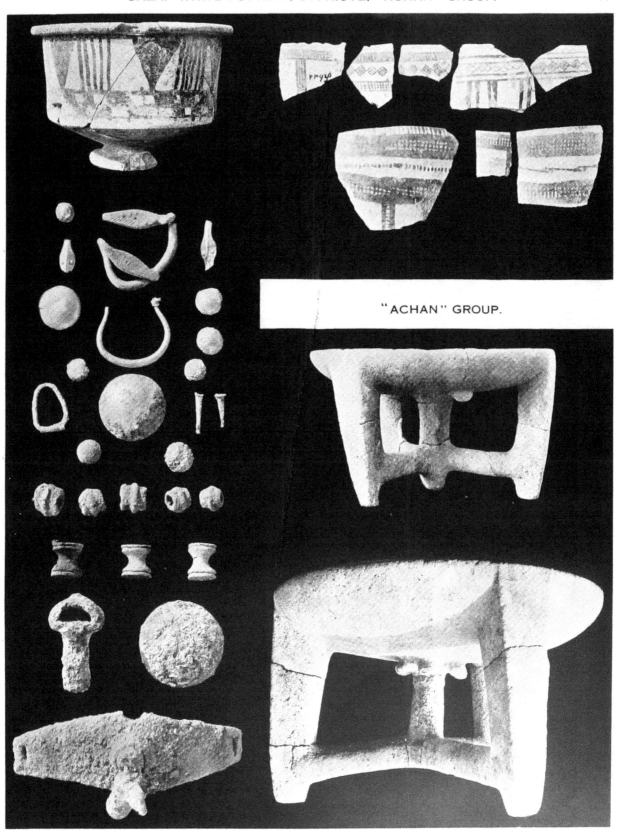

"ACHAN" GROUP.

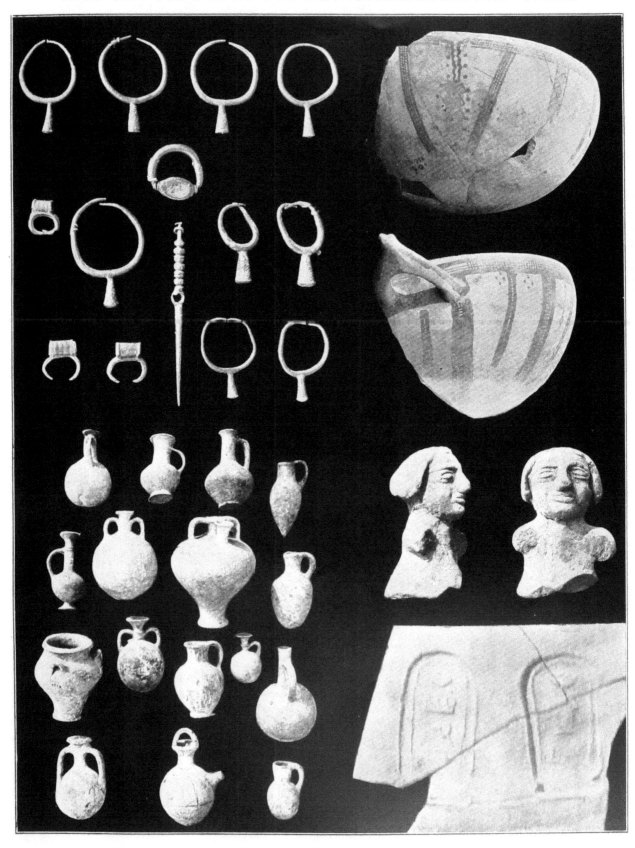

F.P.

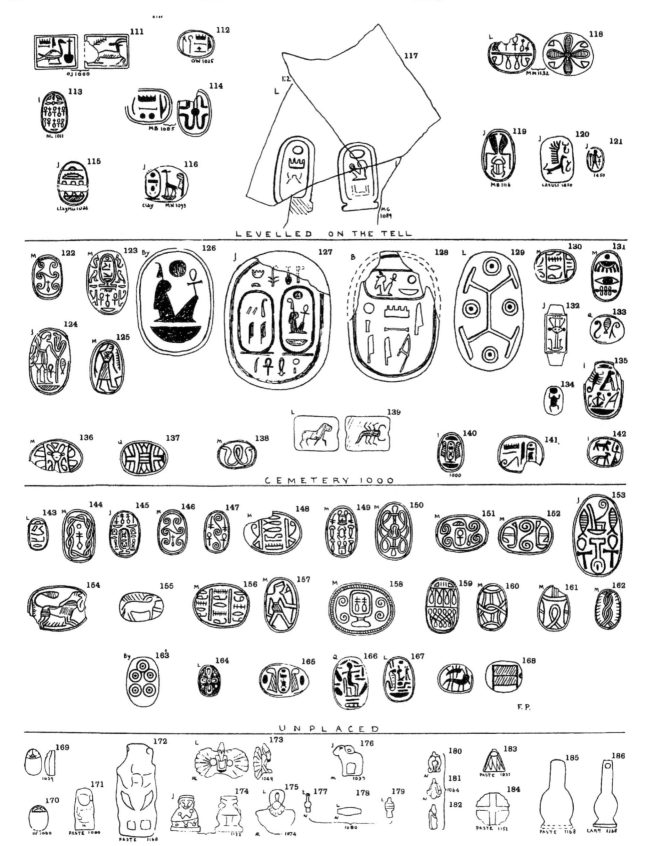

LEVELLED ON THE TELL

CEMETERY 1000

UNPLACED

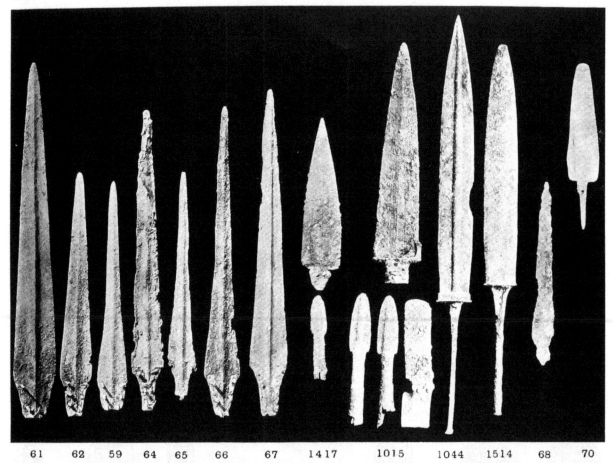

61   62   59   64   65   66   67   1417   1015   1044   1514   68   70

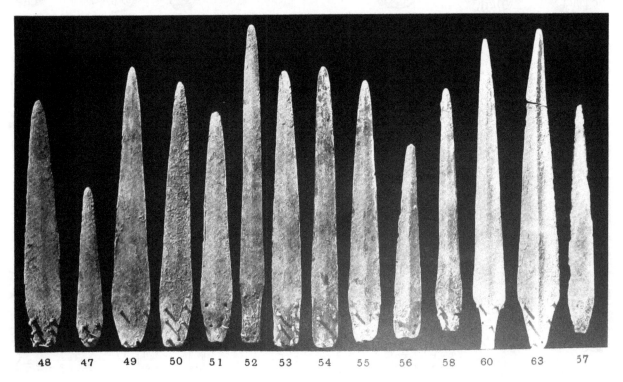

48   47   49   50   51   52   53   54   55   56   58   60   63   57

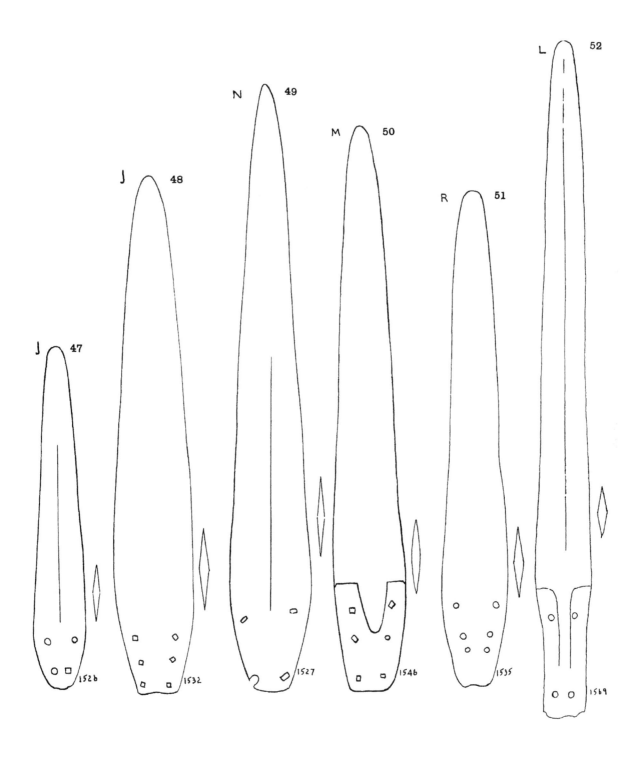

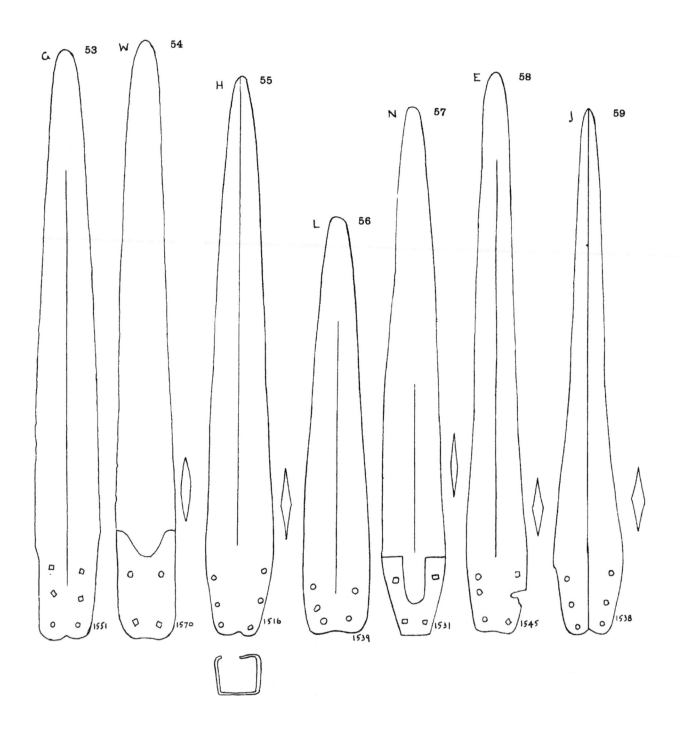

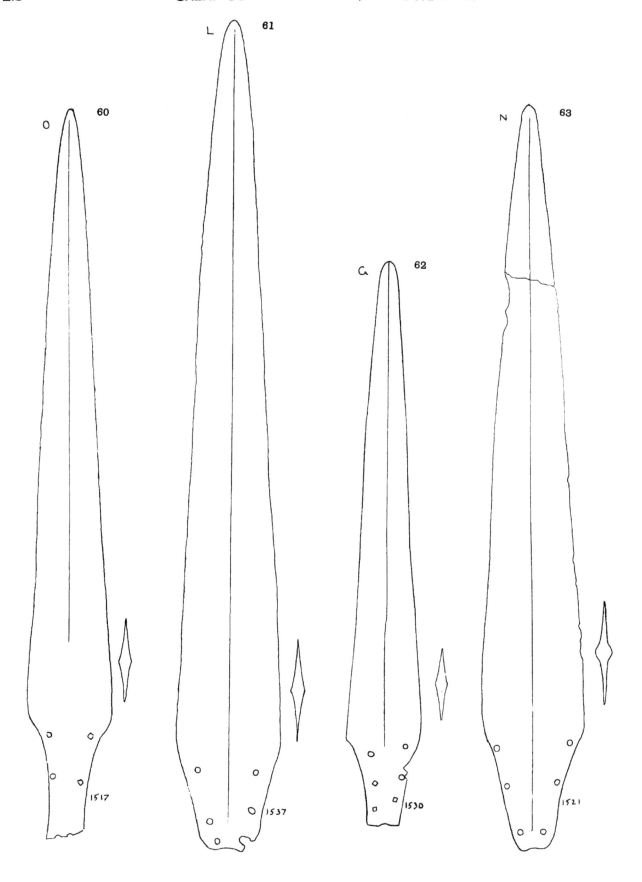

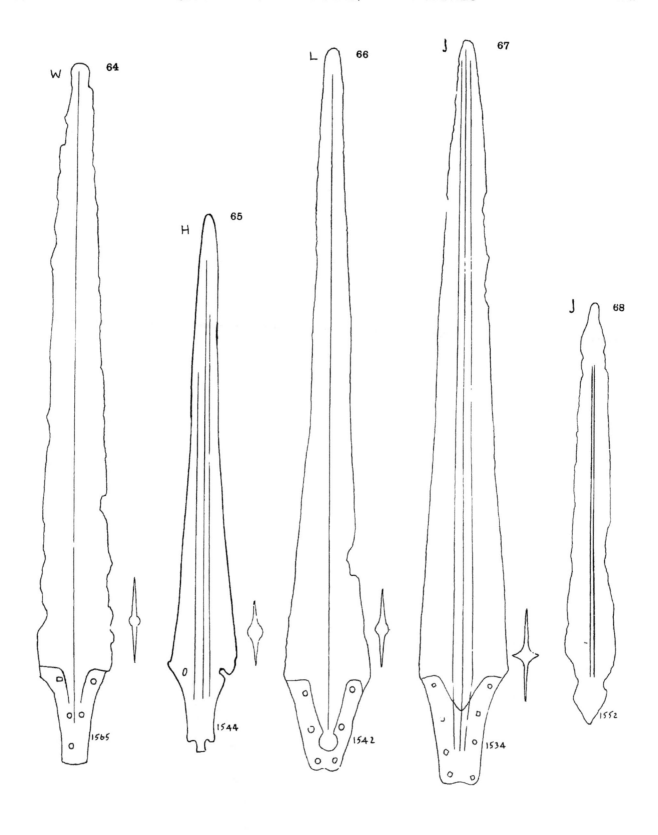

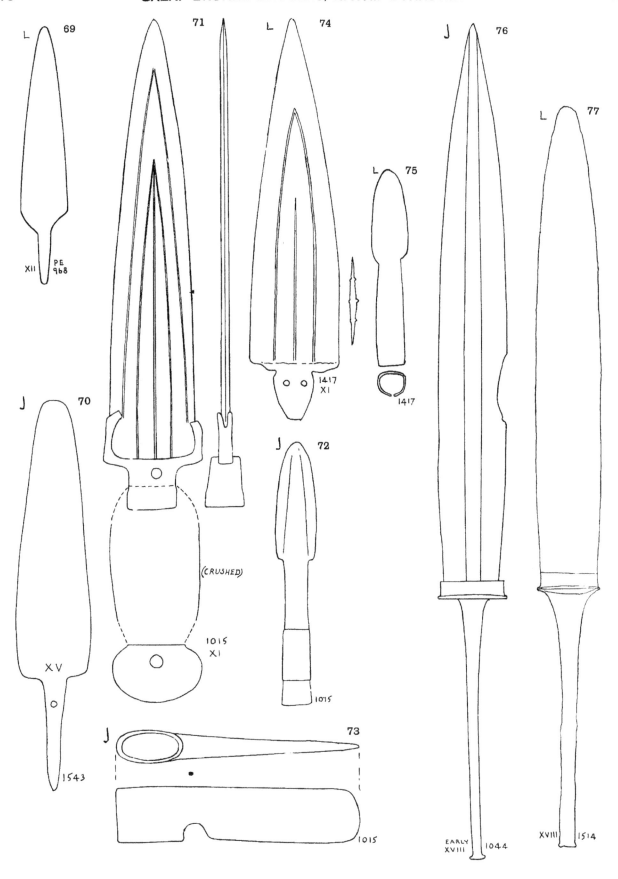

L 69
XII   PE
       968

L   71

L 74

L 75

J 70

(CRUSHED)

1015
XI

XV

1543

J 72

1015

J 73

1015

1417
XI

1417

J 76

EARLY
XVIII   1044

L 77

XVIII   1514

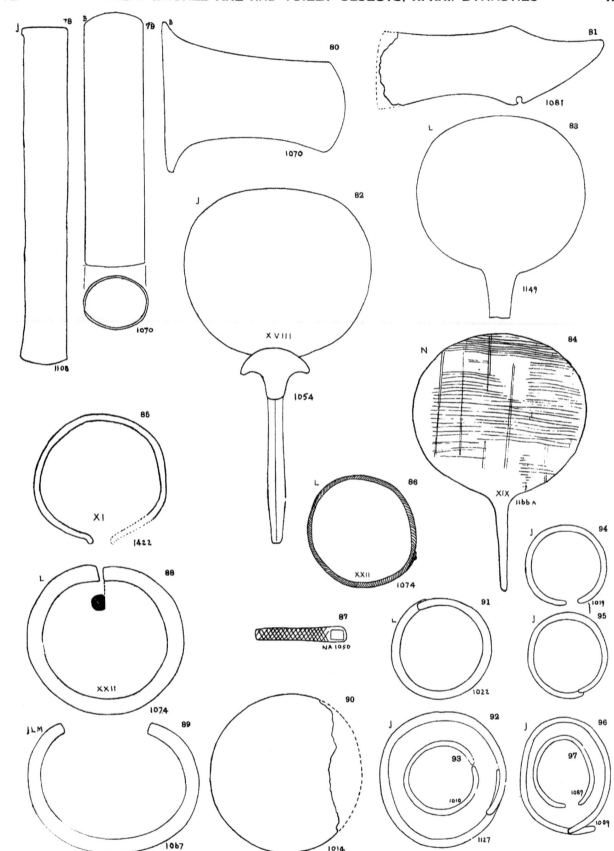

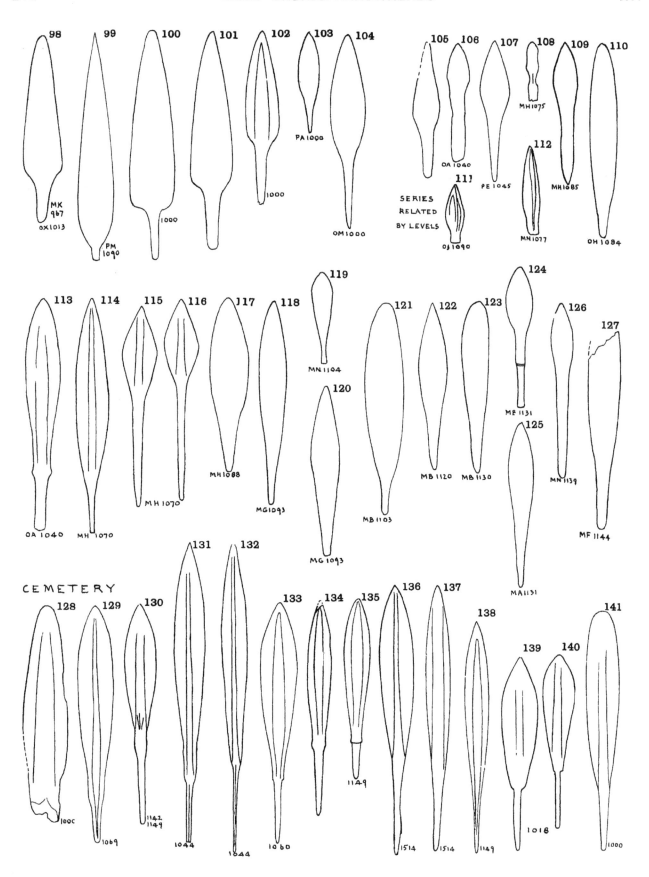

SERIES
RELATED
BY LEVELS

CEMETERY

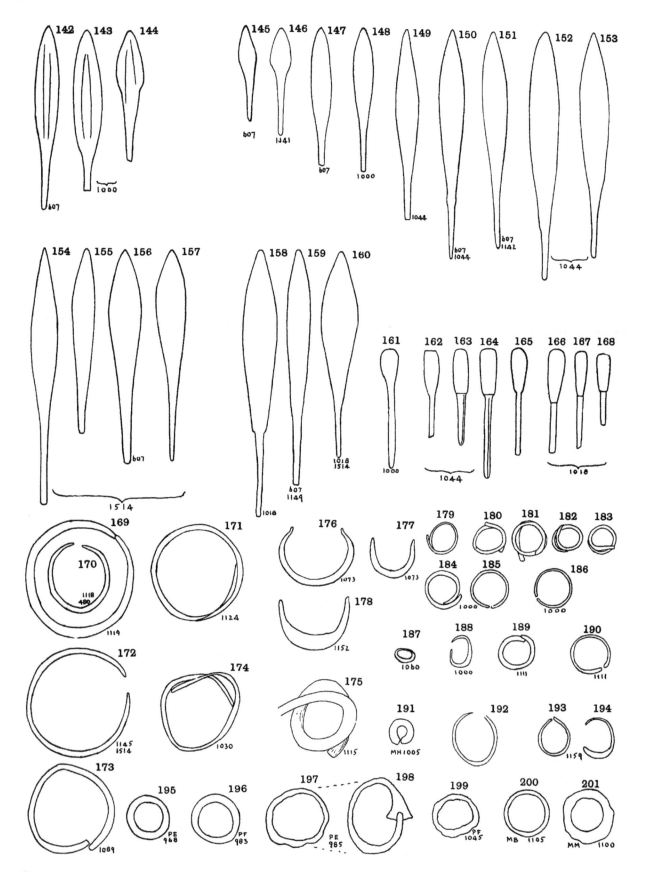

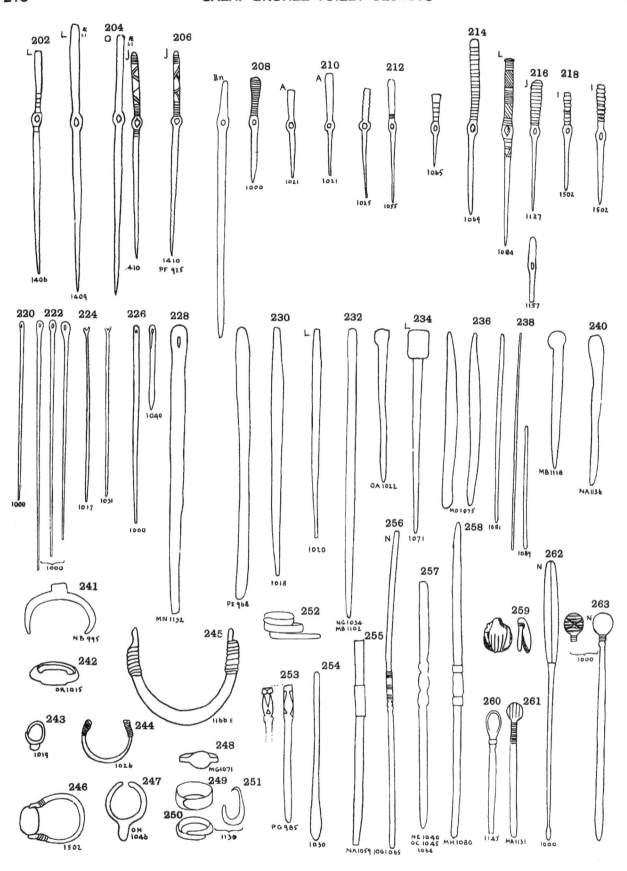

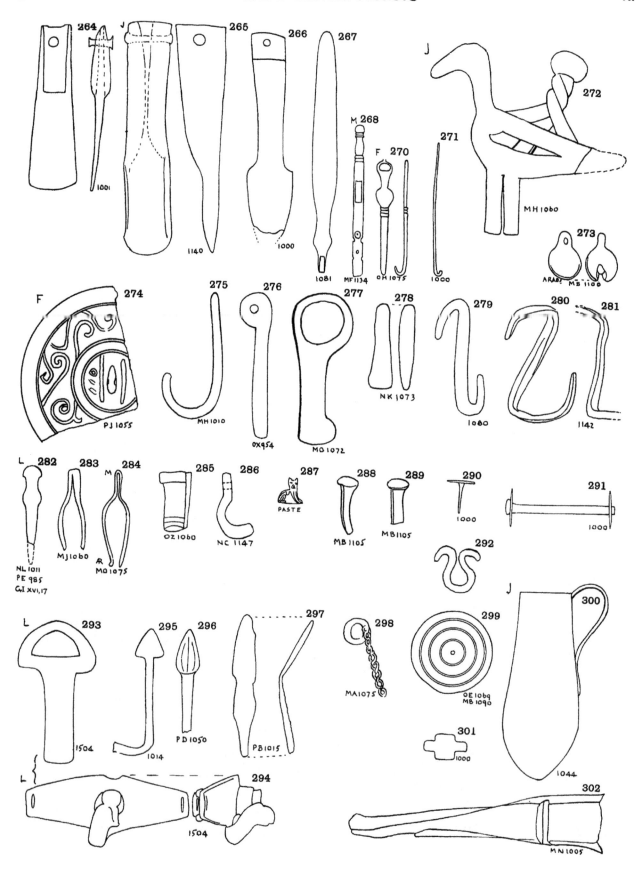

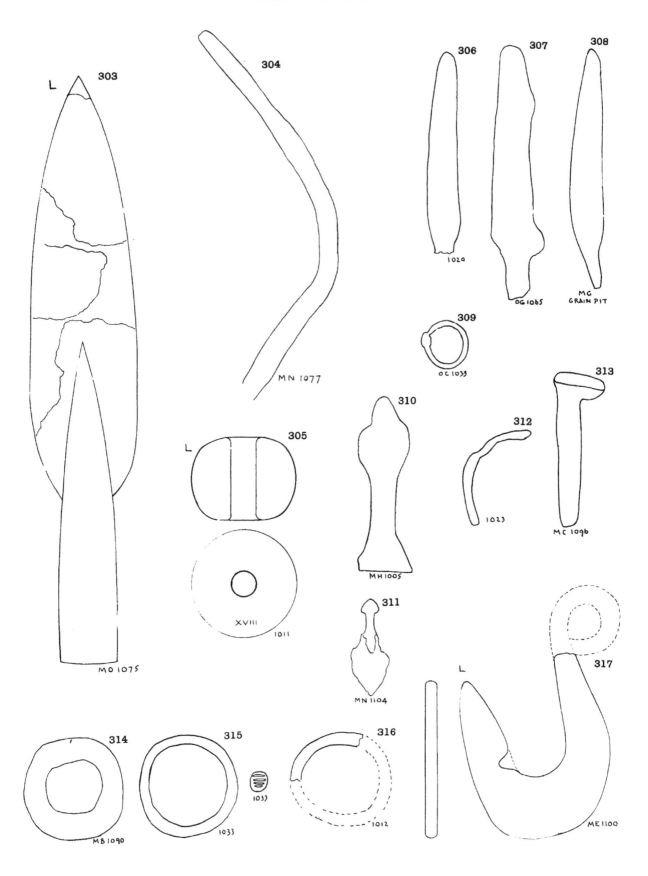

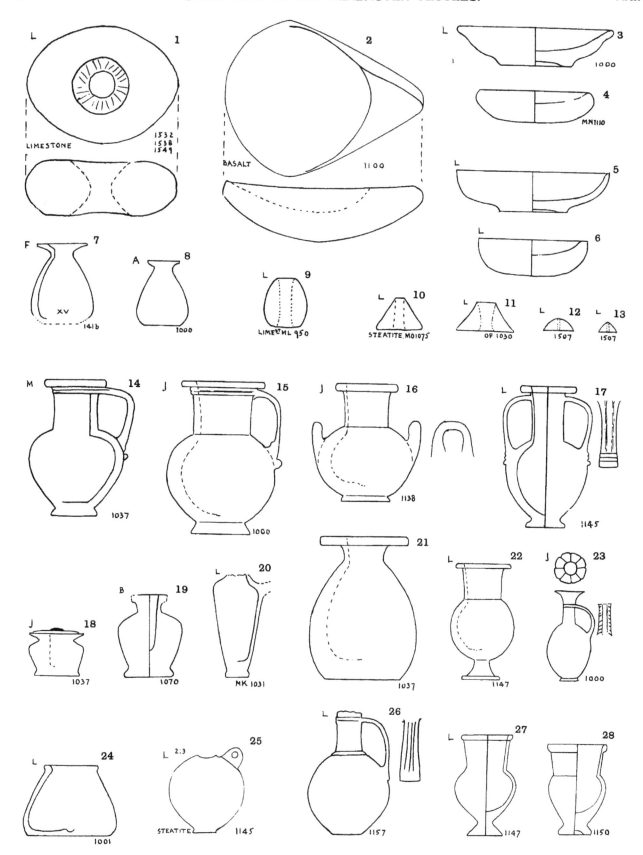

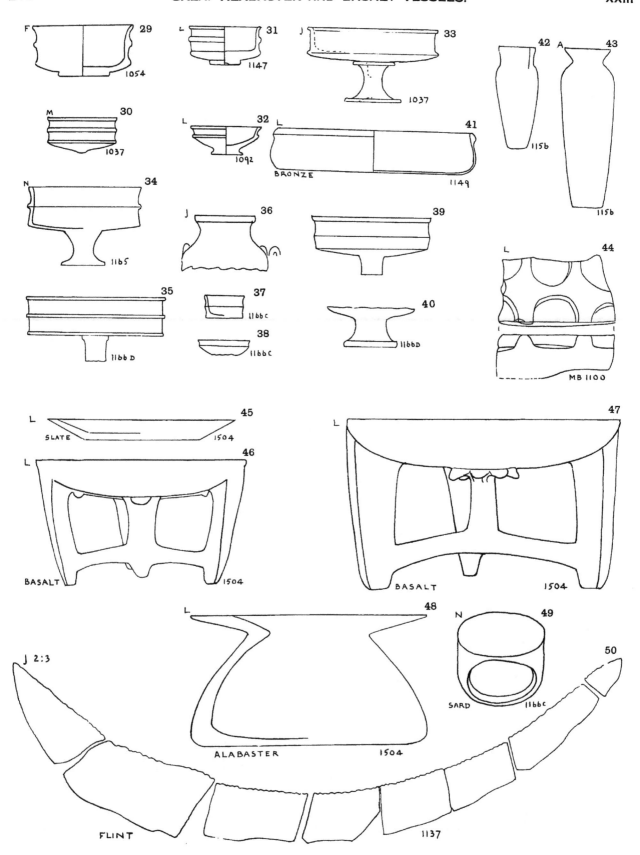

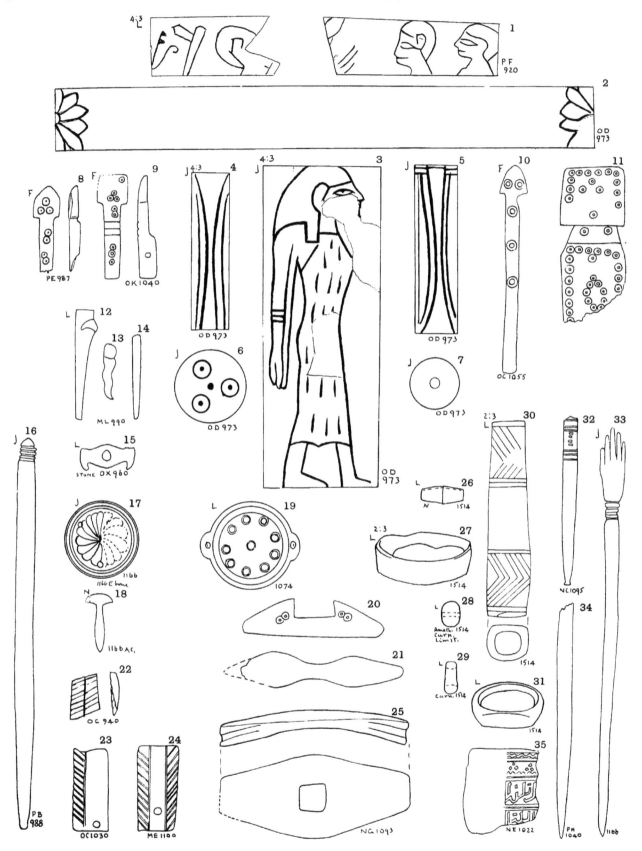

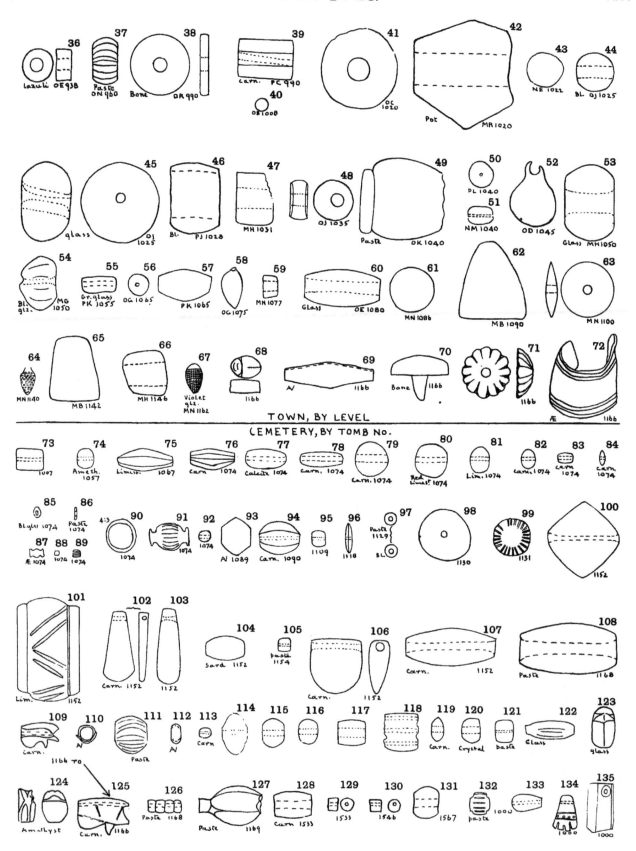

TOWN, BY LEVEL

CEMETERY, BY TOMB No.

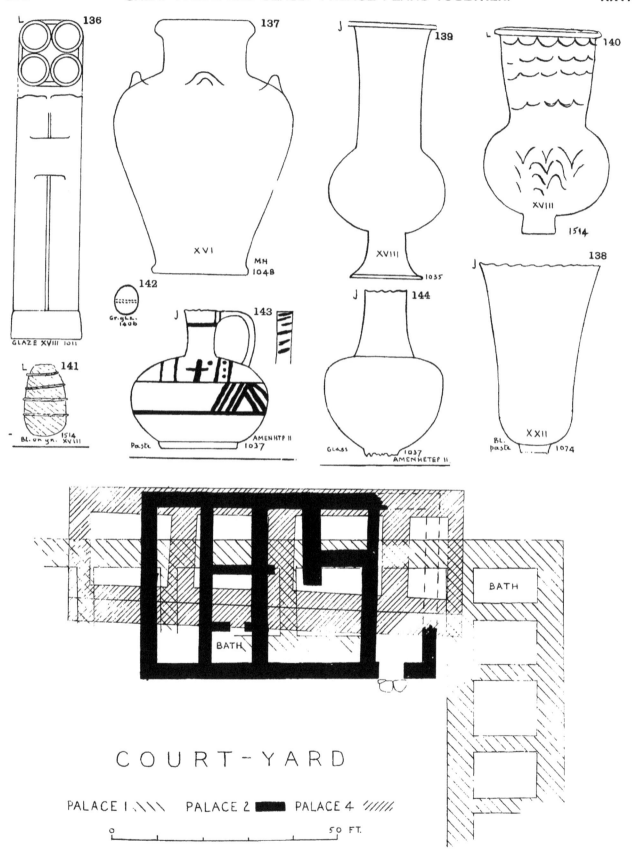

COURT-YARD

PALACE 1 \\\\   PALACE 2 ▬▬   PALACE 4 //////

0   50 FT.

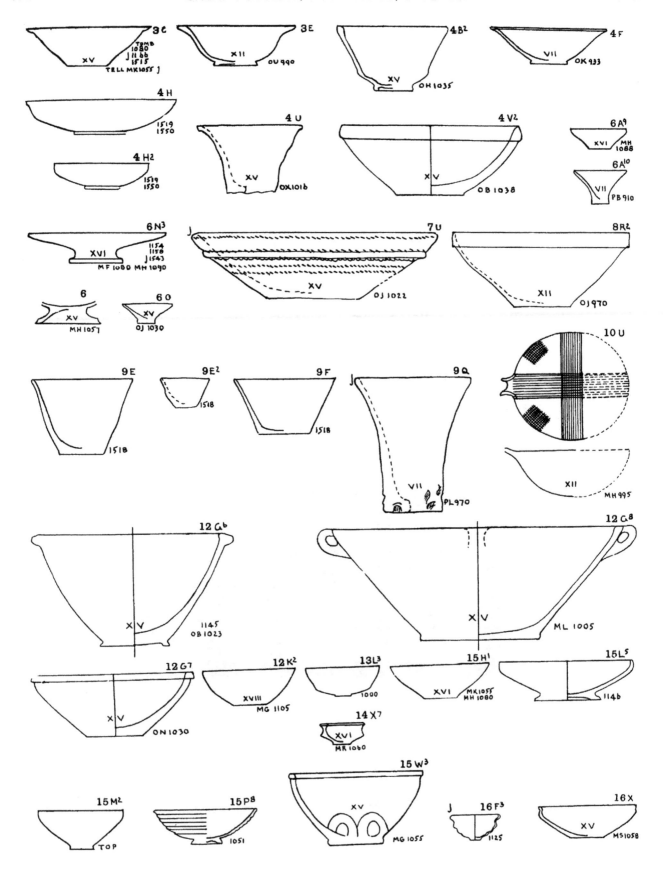

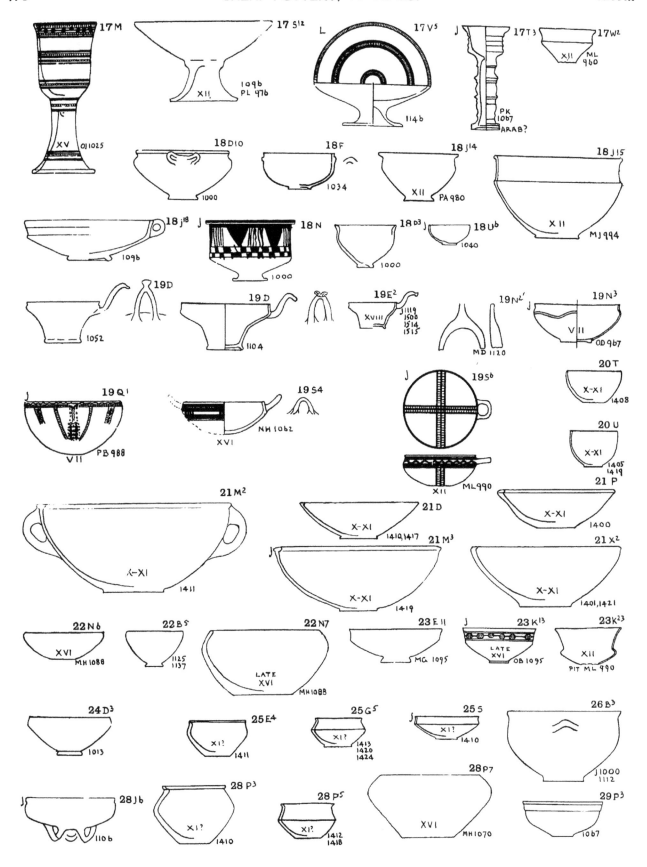

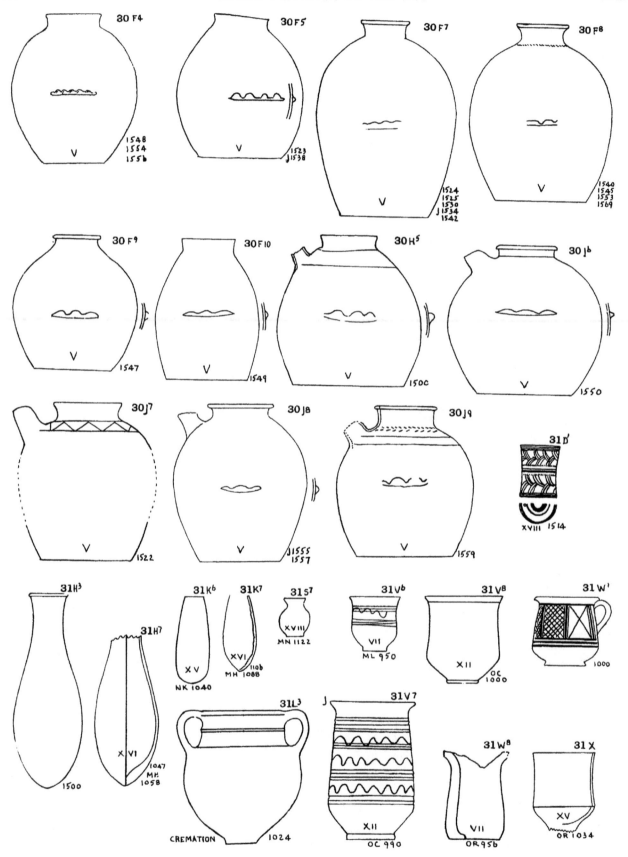

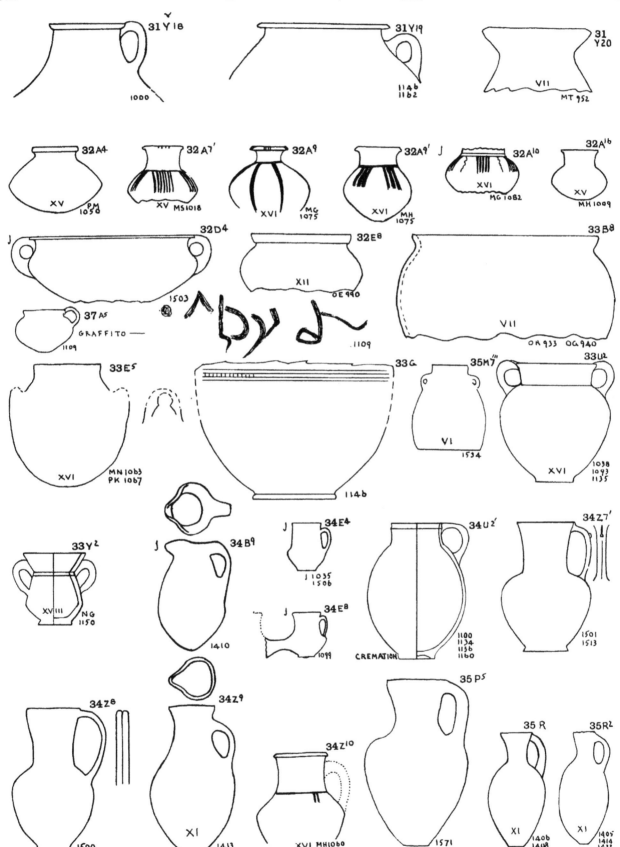

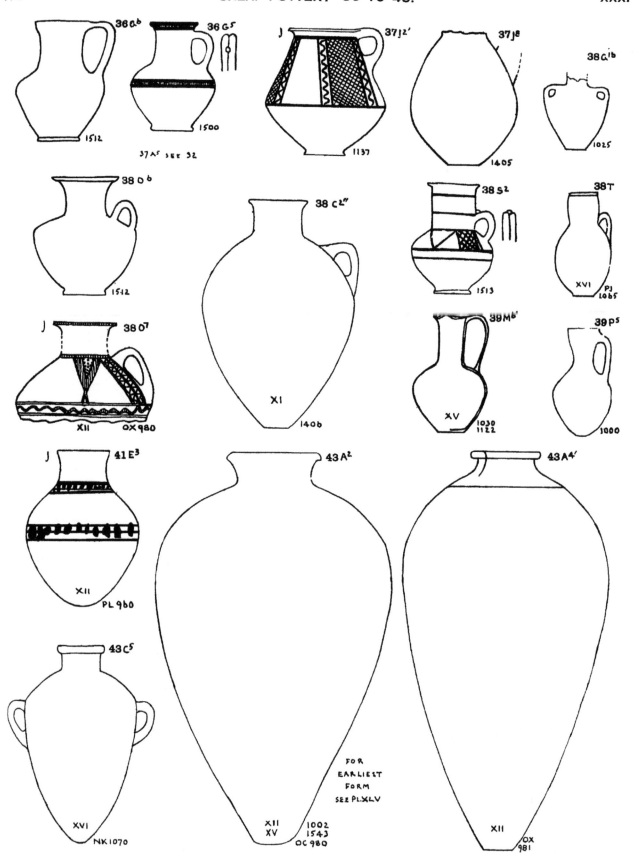

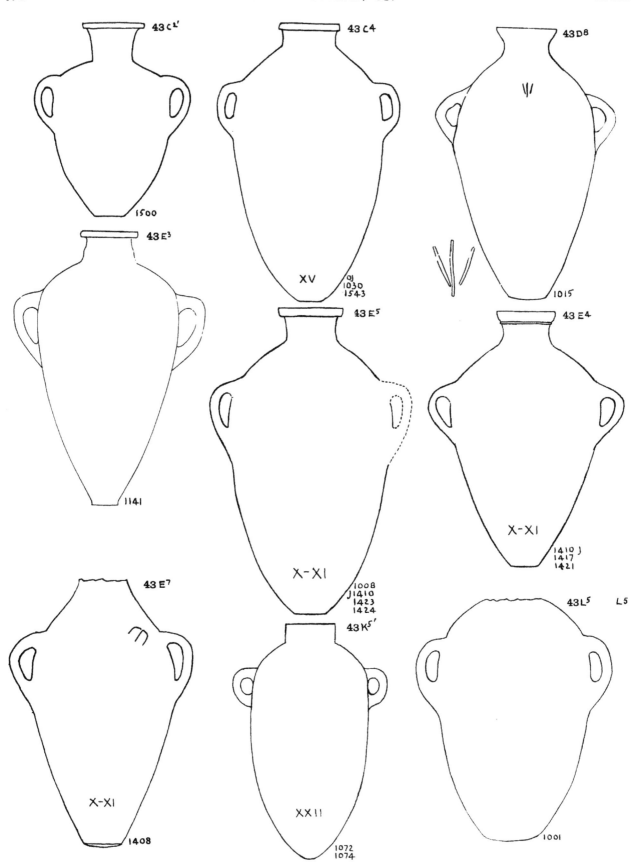

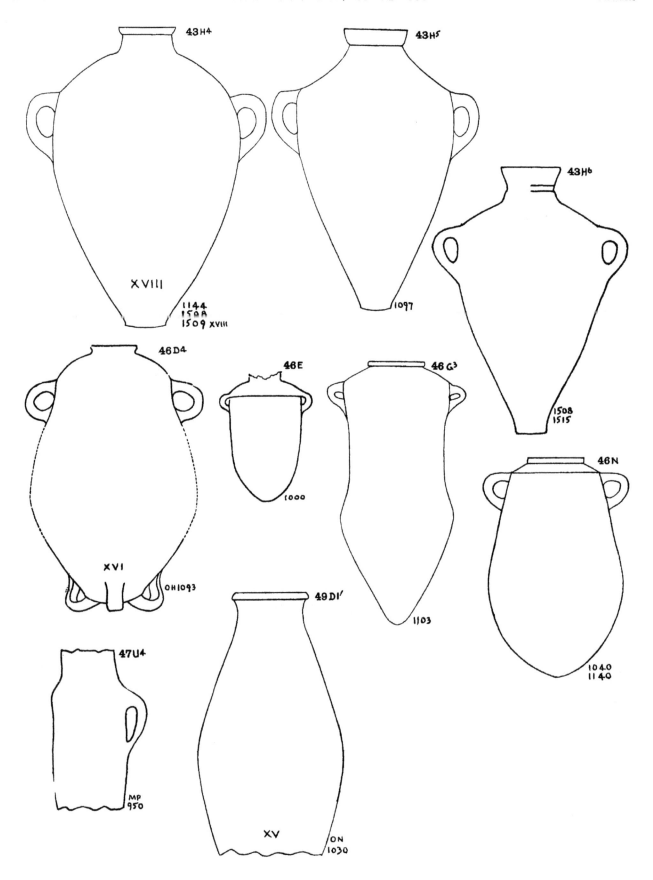

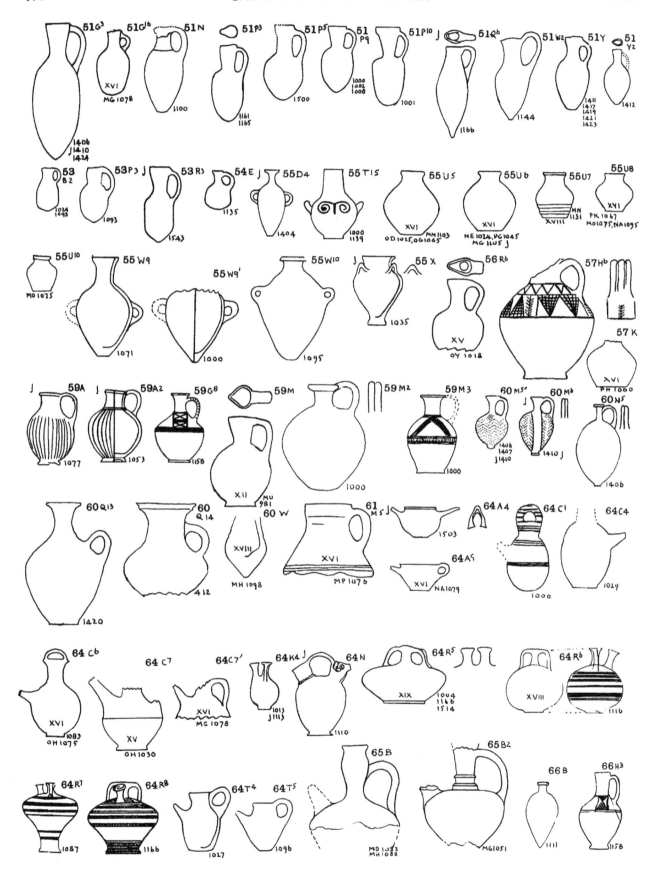

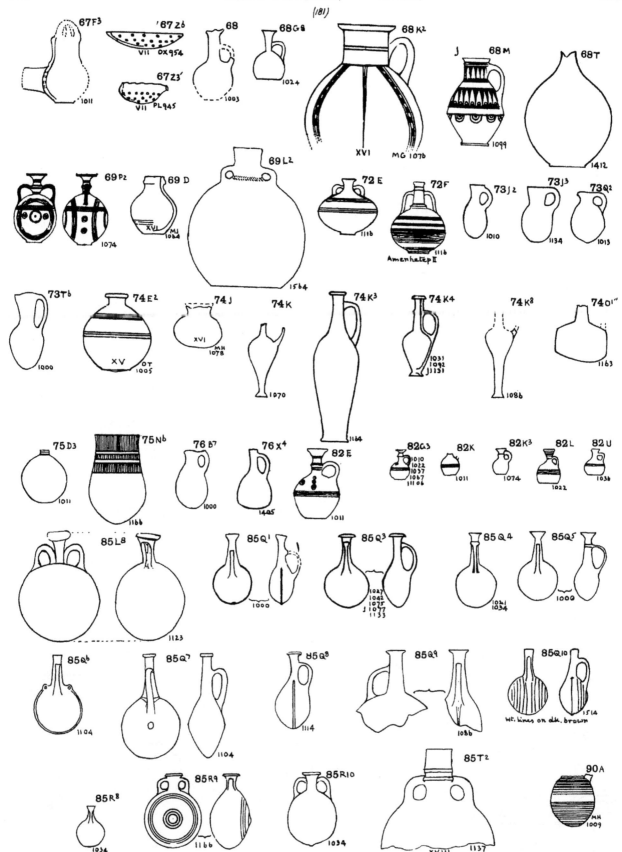

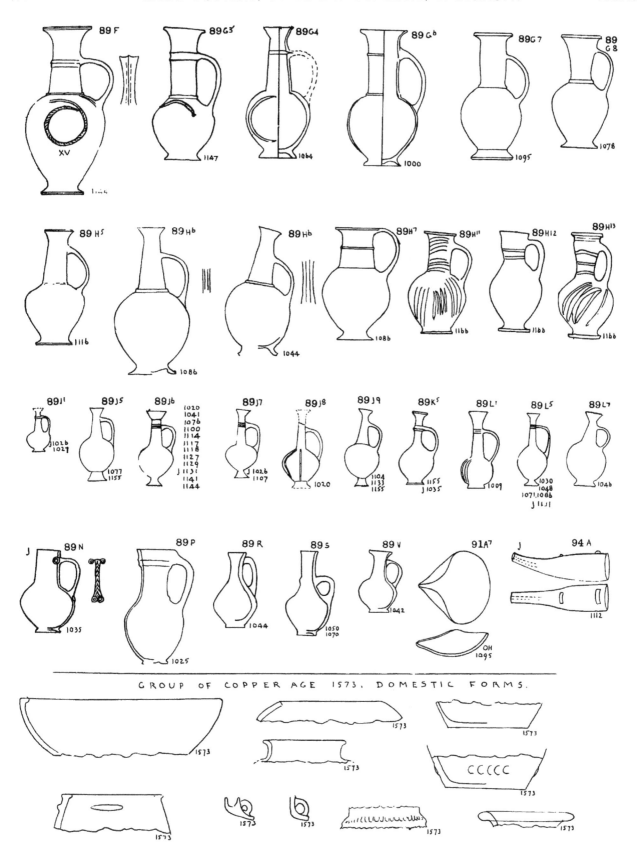

GROUP OF COPPER AGE 1573, DOMESTIC FORMS.

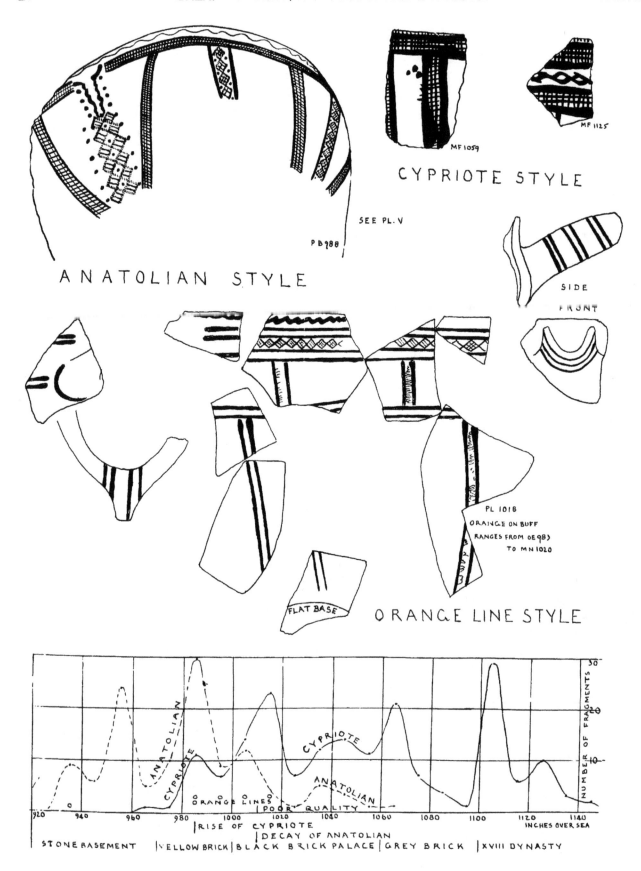

CYPRIOTE STYLE

MF 1059

MF 1125

SEE PL. V

P B 988

ANATOLIAN STYLE

SIDE

FRONT

PL 1018

ORANGE ON BUFF

RANGES FROM OE 983

TO MN 1010

FLAT BASE

ORANGE LINE STYLE

ANATOLIAN

CYPRIOTE

CYPRIOTE

ANATOLIAN

ORANGE LINES

POOR QUALITY

NUMBER OF FRAGMENTS

30

20

10

920 940 960 980 1000 1020 1040 1060 1080 1100 1120 1140

INCHES OVER SEA

RISE OF CYPRIOTE

DECAY OF ANATOLIAN

STONE BASEMENT | YELLOW BRICK | BLACK BRICK PALACE | GREY BRICK | XVIII DYNASTY

	XVIII DYNASTY			GREY BRICK PALACE				BLACK BRICK PALACE						YELLOW BRICK PALACE			STONE BASEMENT PALACE			
	1129–20	1119–10	1109–0	1099–0	1089–0	1079–0	1069–0	1059–0	1049–0	1039–0	1029–0	1019–0	1009–0	999–0	989–0	979–0	969–0	959–0	949–0	939–
Dull br-bk bands						NH		PE, PL				PL			OF					
Dull rd-bk bands		MN	MM, MN	MN, MJ			NK in bowl	MS fine	MN		OJ									
Parallel bands	MN					MN, OH, N		MH						ON				PK		
Parallel lines	NC		MN	MN	MN	MG, OJ	MH	PM	PG MH	MH	MP	MS	OE			PL, MV	OM, PG	MS, OZ		PL, OY
Metopic													OJ	OA	PD, OZ	PL	OF, OM, OY	OY		PE
Parallel rd-bk								MH	ML	MH				MG, ML, OHV	OE		OJ, OY	OZ, PL		MR, OE, OY
White lines on br.		+	MN							PJ			PH							
Parallel barred		MN				MG, OJ late	MK-L, OE OL								PH					
Dabs				ON						PJ	OJ									
Bowls							NH			NJ	MJ, MN		ODB	MH	OE, PD		OF	OL PL		PE PG
Grey shade				MN																
Cross lines				MN		MH		MS NH				OD OJ OR MN	MP PJ		OM PG	MK	OY	PK OY		OY
V lines													MV, OCH ON			MH	OM, OX	OX		
V lines													MH, OCH	NL MLD, MG		PD	MLD		PD	
Wavy					MH		MB, MK	MS	Mg, NH	MH, NH		PL	OF	MG	MNJ, OX PA			PG MT NK PL		MR, OE OG
Vandyke						OH		PD							PG, PH, OX					
Chequers												MH		ML	OE+{1020 940			PG		
Hour-glass				MB								+1090 ON, OP	MH, OJ OP							
Banded															OX	MH	OM			
Plaited						MH VERY ROUGH	OM				CARELESS MA, OA, NA		MH MV, OE	MU, OA	MV NK OS OL	OZ		OJ PF, PG, PL	OM	OE, PF
Union Jack			MN		ND							OS OM		MH, MO OM			OM, OY	PE, PL		PE
Wheel												MP					OX			
Cross								MS	OJ						NK		OX, OY	PF		
Standard																		OZ		
Flower							MH LOTUS								OM					
Fish											MY ROUGH		MV	ML OE	MNJ, OS OX	PG		OY		
Bird					MN						MV, PA	OS PL			MV, OS MNJ	OX	ML	MO		OY
Quadruped						NH						MNJ			OS		PL			
Chocolate + white						OH	MK, MO, PL	NH, PD	PG					PG, PL	ODB, OE OXPG PH	OL, OX	PG PF	PL, OM, OG OX PH	OG MD PF	OG MR PF
Thin white bowl								NH	MN	PJ			MT, OE	OA OE, MS	PG	OY	OJ	MS, PH, PL		MR
Polished white		MN						PJ	MN, NH		MR		OE		MR, OE MN, MP, PH	MV, OY		OY, OZ	MU	
Waggles					MN		MK								MR	PD		PL		
Anatolian fork handle, Cypriote	M·F·MN	MF.G.N	MB·G·M·N OJ	MH	ND OH	MG· OH·J· PL·	PJ MD·F·H·O OK·R PJ	MG·S· MF·H PD·E·L	MH·L·N· OH Mg·N· OF·K PL·	MB NA OK·P·PM· MM·N·S OC PJ	MN OA OC·J·U PF	MT· NE· ODB·R·S· PL MN OC·J·K·L·R PL	MH·V OE·M·N·S·T· PH·K·L·M· OA·N PA·H·J·K·L·	MB·H· OE·M·H PG MB·H·U OM·X PG·L·	MP·R·S· OD·E·LNS·X·Y PBDE·GHL· J PG·H·L·	MH·S·T· OK·Y·Z· PF·H·E· PL	MU OJ·L·Y PD·	MVI OF·J·K·L·M·X·Y·Z PG·H·L	MR·U· OG· PF·	MB·D·R· OE·G·Y·Z PF· PE·
Thin brown			MN	MN					NL	MN	MN, NE			OHV OL				OM, OL, PL		OE COARSE
" " loop	MB, MF								MN	MH					MNJ, MS					PE
" " reliefs								PE	OK				MV	PA MH PG MV			OJ			
" bk+red lines						OJ		MS			ML MN, MNJ		MV, OE, PL	MU	PH MNJ, OK-2	MH	OZ OF, ON, OY	OM		910 PG MR. PF.
Cypriote U spouts	MB												OE		MNJ, MS		OY			
Incised wreaths										OZ			PL	PH	MP	MP				MR

UNDERLINED, KEPT AT JERUSALEM

F.P.

The material originally positioned here is too large for reproduction in this reissue. A PDF can be downloaded from the web address given on page iv of this book, by clicking on 'Resources Available'.

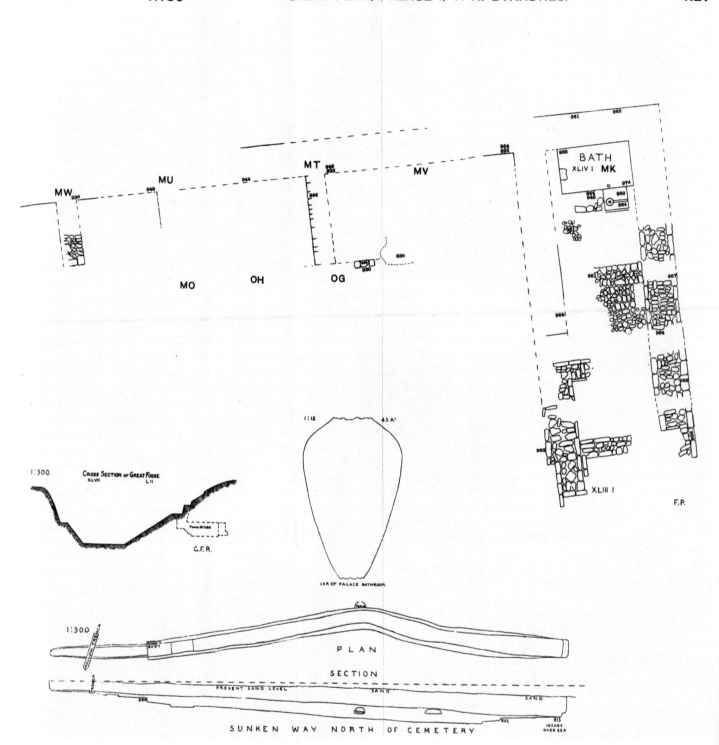

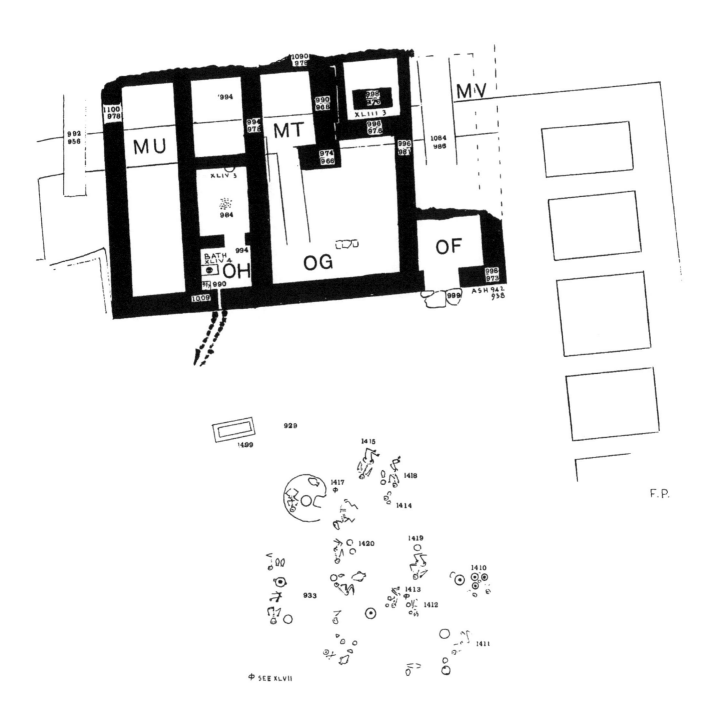

Φ SEE XLVII

1417

1413

The material originally positioned here is too large for reproduction in this reissue. A PDF can be downloaded from the web address given on page iv of this book, by clicking on 'Resources Available'.

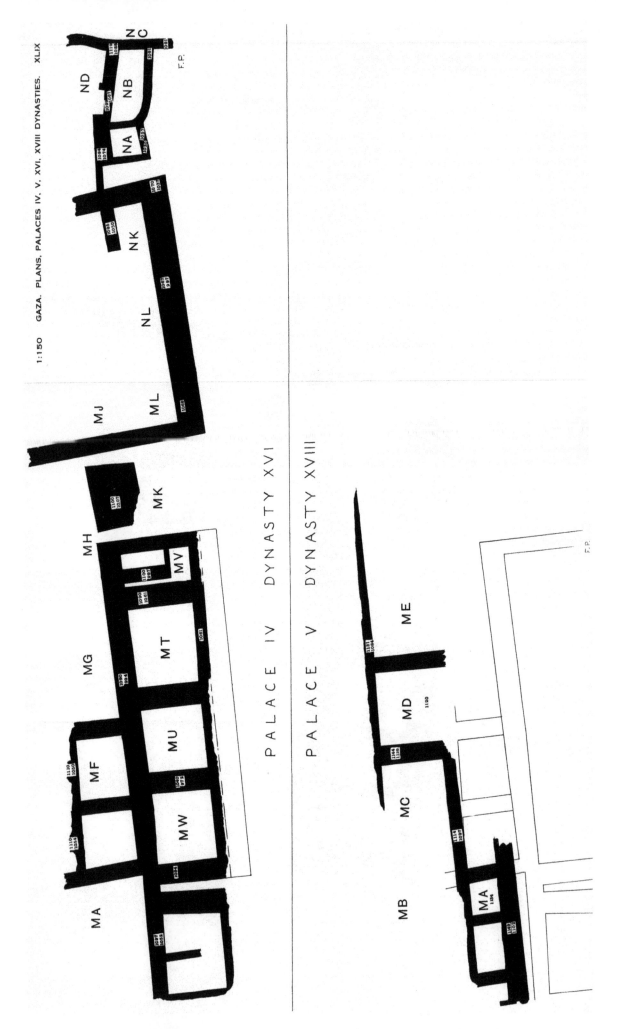

PALACE IV   DYNASTY XVI

PALACE V   DYNASTY XVIII

The material originally positioned here is too large for reproduction in this reissue. A PDF can be downloaded from the web address given on page iv of this book, by clicking on 'Resources Available'.

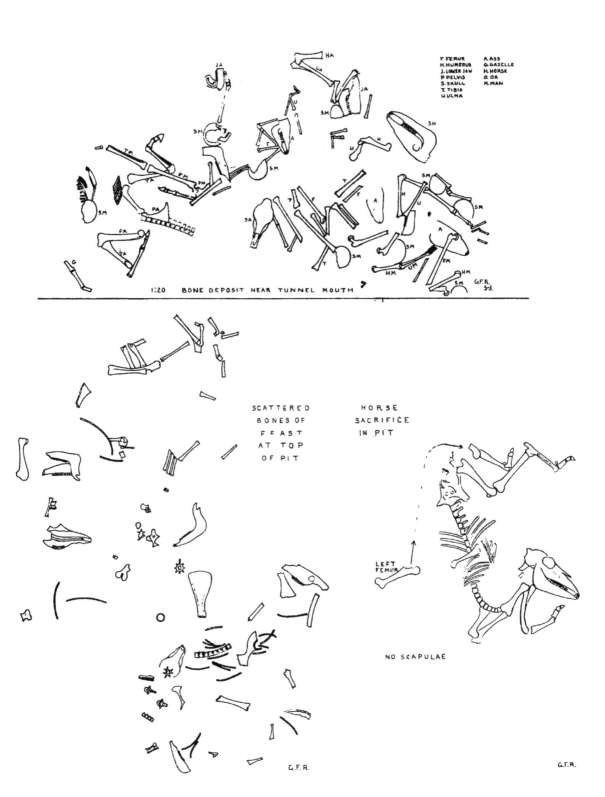

1:20　　BONE DEPOSIT NEAR TUNNEL MOUTH

SCATTERED
BONES OF
FEAST
AT TOP
OF PIT

HORSE
SACRIFICE
IN PIT

LEFT
FEMUR

NO SCAPULAE

G.F.R.

G.F.R.

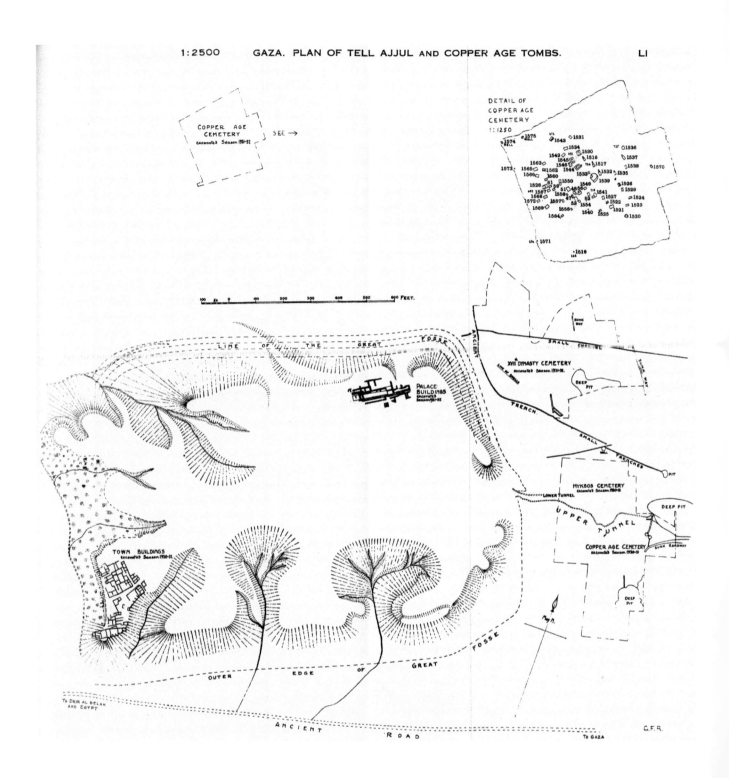

GAZA. PLAN OF CEMETERY, XVIII DYNASTY.

XVIII DYNASTY CEMETERY
Excavated Season 1934-32

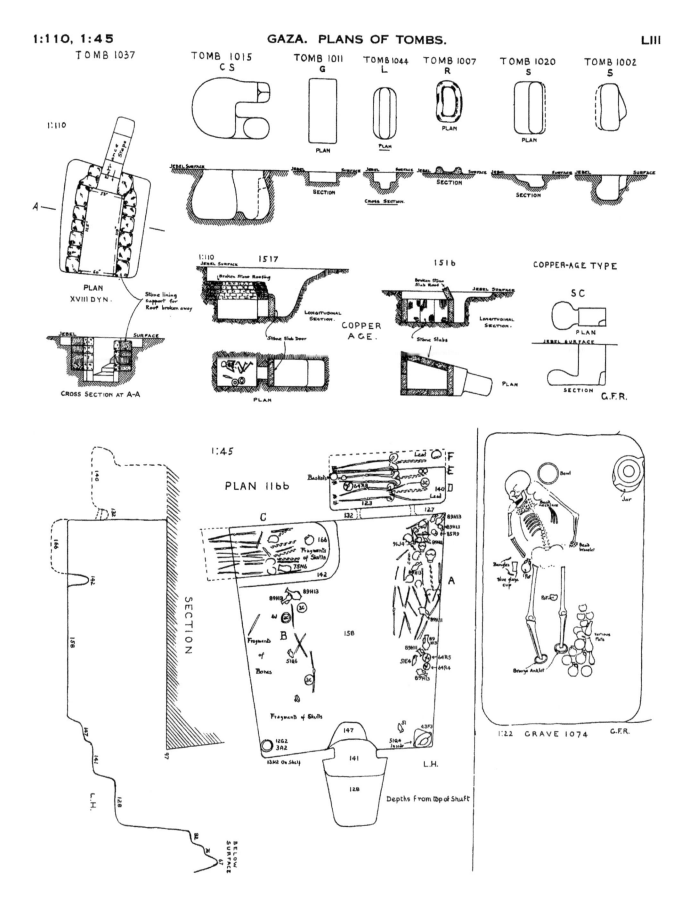

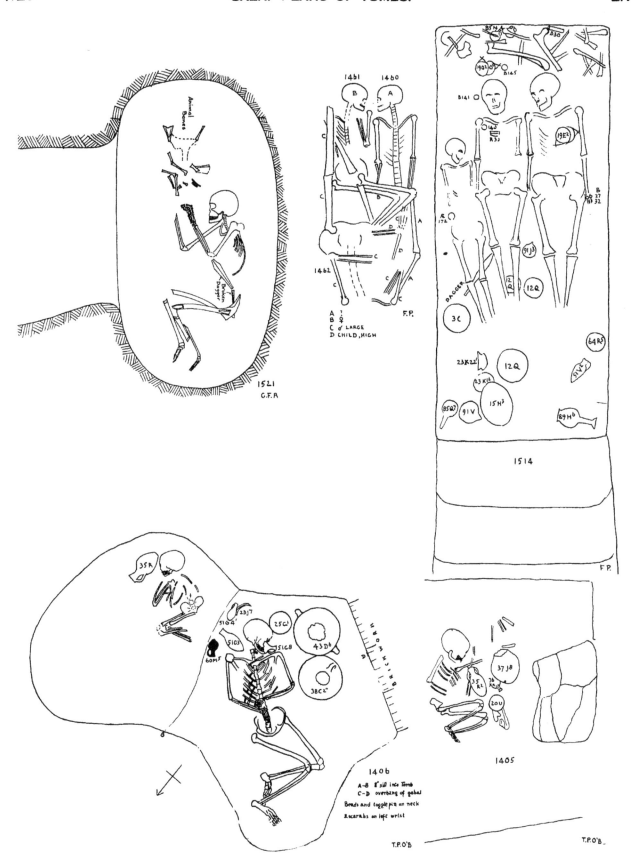

T.N.S.	POTTERY	OBJECTS
1170		
62		B 67
50	13A, NC 33Y² 55U⁴	
46		M 286, B66
44		M 127, 260
42	MB	B65
40		M 126, B64
37	MH85T²	R50
35	MH31H²	M 240
34	NB740"	M 268
32		S118 M 228
31	MN 55 U7	M 124-5, M 261
30		M 123
28	MA6 N⁴	
22	MN 315⁷	(1125) P 41
20		M 122
18		S 119 M 239
15	MG43 D	
13	MH 12 F	
10		R 4
8	NC 51G⁶,10	
6	MN 55 U6	
5	MG10H4, 12K K², L4 MG 55U6	M 200
4		M 119, 311
3	ME 16G4, MN 49R², MM55 U5	M 121, 232
1100	MN 12G² 31 H⁷ MH 60 M	M 201, 273, 317, R 2, 44, B24 63
1895	MG23E", OH23K", NE 89R³, MG 91A¹, G⁴, OH91A¹	M312, B32
93	OH46 D4	S116, M 118, 120, B 25
92		
91	MH 12 G²	
90	MH 6N³, MG12C, K	M 99, 299, 314, B62
89	MH 12 B, C, K, K², M, N4, 22N⁷, 65 8,89J, 91F²	S 117, M 117
7	MN 20N, MH22N5	S 115 B 61
5		S114, M 109
4		M 110, P 7
3	MD 65B	
2	ME MG 32A¹⁰	
80	6N³ MH 15 H¹	M 258, B 60
79	NA64A⁹	
8	MC10H⁴ MG 51G⁶ MG 64G²	
7	MG 12 K MM 315⁵	M 112, 304, B59
6	OH 32A" MP 61M⁵, MG 68K²	
5	MG10K², MH, MG 32 A⁹ MO55 U7,8,10, OH 64C⁶, 91G⁵	M 108, 235-6, R 10
	PA10H⁸ OG 32A⁸	M 270, 284, 298, 303, B19, P 3
3	MH 23K²⁴ MH7AJ	M278
2		M 277
70	MH 12 F, K, R, 16 R, K² 28 P5	M 114-6, 248
69		M 299
8		
7	NA6M, PK 17T³ PK 33E⁵ 55 U⁸	
5	PJ32 S7, 38T, OG 55U5	M 307, B57-8, P29
4	MJ69D	M 256-7
3	MH 23 K¹	P 20
60	MR14X⁷ MN 33 E⁵, MK 34Z¹⁰ NM35 B², PH57K	M 272, 283, 285
	MK 32 A⁹,10,11, 34Z"	M 256, P40
58	OH7W, MS16X, MH31H⁷	P 35
7	PL 12T, PL 15U4, OF 20N	P 13
6	NB 6A⁹	
5	MK 3C, PL10K⁶, MG 15W³ MK15H¹	M 274, B10, 55
4	OE 10 5	
2	OA16 R¹	
1	MG 64 C4, 06, 65 B²	
50	OG 315⁵, PM 32A⁴	M 87, 296, B 54
48	MH 32 A⁹, V.	
7	MH 32 A⁴	M 247
6	OF 15 M³ PG 55 U⁶, ML 55 W7	
5	OF12M PL12K, OD15H⁸ MG31K³	M 107, 199, 257, B52
3	MN 32A⁹	M 256
40	MN 23D, NK 31K⁶, NL 32A⁹	B 9, 34, 49-51
		M 106, 111, 113, 227, 257
38	OB 4V², 12T	
35	OH4 B²	ML 685 B48, P32
34	ON 6E¹³, 31X 12G²	M232

1033	MS 32 A"	M 309
30	ON 12G⁷, R, MP 23 K 25,'" OJ43 C4, ON 49 D¹, OJ60	M 254, B23, 47
	OF32 A⁸, NE 35 H⁹ OH 64 C⁷, NE 35 H⁸	
29	NE 55 U⁶	
8		B 46
	PL 12 M⁶	
5	OJ10H⁸, OJ17M, 23 K³,16,29, OE 39 M⁶, OD55 U⁵	S112, B44-5
	OC 12 K, 13K, OJ18R⁹, T³, OC 31K⁷ O55 D F	B9
3	OB 12 G⁶	M 105, B43
2	OJ7U	M 233, B35
1	OA 51 K²	
20	MN 23 G⁴	R11, B42-3, P42
18	OY6 N³, PC 12K, OZ 23 K¹³ 32 A⁹, OY 32 D⁴, MS 38 A⁷	P 38
17	OM 48Y, MS 50 P	P 1, 30
16	OX 9Q, ML 18J", 195³, 23 K19, K23, OX 315 8, H²	
15		M 242, 297, P 33
13	OY 56 R⁹	M 295, P 10
11		S 113, M 282
10	MK 32 A⁹ 43 F 3, 4	M 275, P 11
7	MH 610²	M 302
5	ML 12 G⁷, 23 K17, MH 23 K²⁵ UT 74 E²	M 191, 288-9, 310
1000	OY 10 E4, 18N, PN 31 L² PH 51 G 4'"	B39-40
	PL 12 F MK 18 K, OCH 31 V⁸	S 111, M 103-4
999	PL 16 R³	
5	MH 10 U	M 241
4	MJ 18 J 15	
2	OA 28 A³	
90	OU3E, ODE 19F, MS 23 K¹⁹ OCH 31 V7, MH 32 D⁴, OE 32 E⁹	B 12-14, 38-39 P18, 19, 26
89	OD 19F' MS 23 K 25'"	
8	PB 19 A¹	B16, P21, 39
7	OD 19 N³ OY 5T 5²	
5	MJ 16 R², OE 18 K² NK 23 E¹⁰	M 197-8, 253, P17, 25
3	PA 18 J¹⁴ MH 32 A⁹	M 15, 19 6, P 15
1	OJ 8 R² OX 43 A4¹, MU 59 M	
80	MK 10 E9", OH 10K8, PL12C, 19F³, OB 23J¹⁵, OX 38 O⁷ OC 43 A"	P 8, 37
78	MV 23 K¹⁸	
6	PL 17 S¹²	B2-7
70	O58 R³, PL 9 P, Q, 17 B4¹, PL 41 E³	P 16
	PM 13 G 4 OK 18 J³	
67		M69, 98, 195, 229 P 23
6	OR 31 W 2	P 2
5		
4	OX 672⁶	
2	MT 31 V²⁰	
60	OY 6 N⁴ ML 12 Y, 19 F¹ 31 V⁶	B 15, 37, P6, 32
	ML 6 N⁵, 6C, 17 W², MP 23 K¹⁶ 47 U⁴	
56	PH 12 T4	
5	OE 23 K¹⁸ PL 67 23¹	M 276, P 24-5
50	PG 23 K²⁹ OY 31 V⁸ OJ 32 A	R9, P 24
47	OM 23 K 25"" OJ 96 W⁶	
3		P 28
40	MR 6 C², OE 23 B4, 23 K¹⁴ OG 33 B⁹	B 22
39	OJ 6 E4 MR 18 J⁵, MR 23 K 25, 16	
8	MOI 6 C4	B 36
33	OK 4 F, 6 C², 18 J¹⁶, K, MU 32 A OR 33 B⁹ MU 43 A³, MP 51 G¹⁴	P 31, 42
29	OY 6 E4, 14, OG 23 K²⁴'''	
25	OG 18 J³	920 B1
14	OZ 6 E¹⁴ PG 60	
13	PG 10 P5	
10	PG 6 A¹⁰, 15 G, 15 K²	
895	PO 15 K²	

TWO LETTERS,   NUMBER + LETTER   S SCARABS   PLS. VII, VIII
= POSITION   = TYPE OF POTTERY   M METAL   PLS. XIV-XX
ON PLANS   IN CORPUS   R ROCK   PLS. XXII-III
PLS XLV-XLIX   PLS. XXVII-XXXVI   B { BONE XXIV / BEADS   PLS. XXV
P PAINTING   PLS. XXXVII-XL

F.P.

No.	TOMB N. E. D.	BODY H F DIST	θ	TYPE	DYN.	POTTERY	SCARABS	METAL	STONE	BEADS	MUS.
1001	24 24 36			G		43 L⁵ 51 P¹⁰			24	BONE GLASS	L
2	64 74 32			S	XV	6F 19F² 23K⁸ 43A⁴ 51P9 F²					
3	22 60 31			S		16K² 68CA²					
4	⊕			G		64R⁵					
5	⊕	W UP O		G	XVI		1				
7	60 37 9	S W ·O		R	XVI	68A⁵	2	207, 222		73	Bn
8	60 26 18	E UP O		G		43E⁵ 51P9 68A⁵					
9	⊕			G		10K² 89L¹					
10	⊕			G		73J² 82G³		93		+	
11	94 43 15			G	XVIII FE	32E² 75D³ 82E,G	3, 4	305		136	L
12	⊕			G	FE			316			
13	⊕			G		15M 24D³ 04K⁴,73Q²					
14	60 30 12	E UP O		G		23A,E²		90 NAIL			
15	88 66 72	E N O		C		43D⁸		71-3			J
16	85 36 12			G						+	J
17	⊕			G				224			By
18	⊕			G				{139-40,158-66 {166-8,230			
19	66 18 12	E UP		G				94-5, 243			J jL
20	75 20 19			G	XV	89J⁶	5	231			A
21	82 14 7	S UP O		G		74K 85Q³		209-10			L
22	⊕	CREM.ᴺ		POT		35E 82G³		91			
23	95 46 20	NW NE O		G	FE	34G 82L'83N²		312			
24	96 30 27	CREMATION		POT		31L³ 53 B² 68G⁸					
25	60 20 16	W		G		38G¹⁶ 89P		211			
26	84 18 18	S UP		G	XVIII	89J, J7	6	244			J
27	66 14 14	S E O		G		64F⁴ 89JG³					
28	66 14 14	S W		G		89M					
29	40 33 6			G	FE	34P² 64C⁴	7	306			Bn
30	78 18 24			S	XV	10K⁸ 39M⁶ 89J, L⁵	8	174 254			By
31	72 24 24			G		68A²·74K⁴		225			
32	54 28 30			S			9				
33	66 18 18			G	FE	85Q⁴,R¹⁰		315		+	
34	40 24			G	XVIII	18F 85Q⁴,R¹⁰	10 11				M
35	105 27 17	S UP O		S	XVIII	12B 31W,34E⁴ 55X 89H²,K⁵,N	12-16, 183		ALAB.	139	J
36	72 19 24	W UP		G	XVIII	82U	17; 18				J
37	123 56 50			C	Aᵐ II	51G⁴ 89J 91M²	19 176	30-3, 116-60	14,18,21 30, 33	+	J,M
38		CREM.ᴺ		G	XVI	33U²					
39	18 60 12	S UP		G	Aᴿ II	85Q⁴,R¹⁰	20 169				R
40	42 14 24			G		16T4,18U⁶ 46N 59R					
41	90 18 6	S W UP O		G	XVIII	23T³ 89J⁶	21				j
42	15 95 15			G	EARLY XVIII	15L² 85Q³,87V, 91K¹		{76,131-2,149-53 {162-4. 300			
44	34 76 24	S W UP Q		G	EARLY XVIII	89H⁵,L³, RK⁴					
46	74 16 12	S W UP		S		89H³, L⁷					
47	73 15 6	N W O		G		31H⁷ 55V³					
48	53 15 13			G		89M		39			
49	72 22 16	E S Q		S		33U 53H	22 173				L
50	16 63 7			G		12G² 89J,L⁵					
51	88 17 15	S UP O		S		12L⁴,P,15 P⁸ 89J					
52	75 16 22	S W		G		19D					
53	90 13 12			S		59A² 89H¹					J
54	15 90 30			G	MID XVIII	51K² 89H		82	29		jf
55	30 81 21	S W UP Q		S	T. III	89J	23-4	212			J
56	19 72 6	S W E O		G		64R³ 69P² 85Q 89K¹					
57	18 63 12	S W N O		G	Aᴿ III	82K²	25-31			74	B
59	23 78 22			S				187			
60	15 57 21	NE		S			170				
61	18 63 30			G		12Q 89U¹ 91K³					
62	54 15 10			G	T. III	89K²	32-3			+	M
64	30 72 24			G		12M,19 P² 82R 89G⁴·K²	180-2			+	
65	24 66 23			⌐		213					
66	72 72 27			PIT		12R 55V 82C,G³⁴		89		75	Ljm
67	100 36 25			G		29P³ 82C,G³⁴		89		75	Ljm
68	18 60 21			G	XVIII		34-6	214			J
69	19 72 25			G				214			
70	24 24 30	S W		G	XVIII	43G⁵ 53A¹ 74K 89J,L³	37-8	114-6,80,129	19		L
71	56 18 12			S	Aᴿ II	55W9 89J, L⁸A	37-8	234			L
73	9			G	XVIII	89G⁴	39-41	24,36,38,176-7		+	JL
74	48 85 30			G	XXII	16F 43K⁵ 69P² 73W4 82G³⁴,K³	42-3 175	86, 88		19 ^6-92	Ljr
75	82 24 14	W UP		G		85Q²,⁰91²					

F.P.

No.	TOMB N E D	BODY H.F. DIST	TYPE	DYN	POTTERY	S SCARABS	M METAL	R STONE	B BONE &c	MUS.
1076	27 84 30		S						+	
77	51 118 36		G		34E² 51K³,53X³,55X³,59A 85Q².3, 89J¹·⁵M					
78	18 72 10 SW N O	G			89G⁹H³					J
79	28 102 39		PIT		33U 82G⁴ •					
80	42 112 60		C	XVIII	3C 55X³ 89H	44.177-9	22,129-60,279			J
81	33 81 12		L				81 237,267			J,Q
82	27 78 27 SW UP O	G	XVIII	19P 38H¹⁰ 51K² 89H¹	45				
83	22 45 16		S		64C⁶	46-7				Bn
84	21 75 21		G		89K⁵		215			L
85	9 60 21 SW UP O	L	XVIII	35Q⁹ 50D²' 74K⁸ 85N⁵89H²·J⁶ 2 plain	35		+	B
86	84 18 40 SW		S							
87	9 45 9		G	T.IV		48-50				Bn
88	9 70 10				85Q²	51	17, 25		+	J,R
89	12 51 10 SW		G		55W⁷ 64K²·N³		18,45,96-7,173		93	J
90	15 72 10 W UP		G		89H¹				94	
91	33 84 12 E UP O	G			22C³ 23K¹ 85J11					
92	36 90 36				74K4			32		
93	CREMATION		R	A.III	32U² 51 P³		ARROW			
95	28 83 24 SW		G		12L⁴ 23K¹⁸ 52E 55W¹⁰ 91H 89G⁷	52-3	22			A
96	33 84 54 SW UP O	G		10K⁹,11J4,17S¹,18J18 64T⁵ 89H¹ 9H²L					
97	O O		R		19P3,4 43H² 51K² 91M²					
98	17 80 27		S		64R4					F
94	36 84 27 SW		G		34E⁸ 68M 85J9Q²89K					J
94	12 39 8		G				18			J,M
1100	27 63 36		G		16M 33D⁵,34U² 51M,52E,53C¹M 73W¹,83B⁵ 89J6					M
1	36 72 16		G		20L³ 64H4	54				M
2	CREMATION		R		36H¹					
3	50 84 42		G		13L² 26R4 46G³,52N²					L
4	8 24 NE SW		G		19D² 51G4 85Q⁶·⁷,89H¹,K	55-8, 64				M
5	O O		R		BULL					M
6	16 90 CREMATION		S		28J6,31K,33D⁴,U 82G³	59				J
7	8 24		R	XVIII	51G7' 89H²J⁷	60	43			J
8	8		R		79					J
9	15 60 18 W		G		10K² 37A⁵ 91F²	61			95	L
10	14 68 12 SW SE O	R			50F 64N 89H¹JK	62 64	46			J
11	24 60 24		G		66B		189-90			
12	69 15 22 SE NW	G		23J¹²,26B³24Q 94A					J
13	125 60 18 E W	G		22N² 64K4 85J³					J
14	15 78 39		G		51E4,64' 85J⁷Q⁹,89J²L					
15	15 72 32 W E	G		16S⁸ 91F²		175			
16	15 110 28		G	A.II	64R⁴,69P²,72E 89H³,5	63				J
17	30 69 36 SW UP O	G	T.III	89J⁶,K⁵	64 65	37 43			M
18	12 60 15 W UP O	R		89J6		170		96	
19	63 63 36		PIT		19E² 59A²,64K³		169			J
20	CREMATION ASII21		•			66				L
22	33 84 36 W UP O	L		39M⁶ 89H¹					
23	15 66 24 SW UP O	R		50F 85L⁰89H²		26			
24	84 84 27		G		17E 171					J
25	15 48 24		G		16F³,22B5 36B³' 85J¹					J
26	CREMATION				15M 84E,85H7					
27	31 86 24 S W O	G	A.III	89H¹J⁶K²	67-8	92,216		+	J
28	84 24 36 W UP O	G	A.II	69-70					J
29	15 66 18 SW UP O	L		89J6				97	
30	60 18 27		G		249-51			98	
31	30 84 36 W UP O	L		225 51K² 74K4 89H¹J⁶L⁵				99	J
32	18 36 18		G	XVIII	85R²L	71			+	F
33	18 84 27 SW UP O	G		51G² 85Q³,89J9					
34	CREMATION				34U² 73J³					
35	CREMATION				18U⁴20L¹ 33U² 54E 83H²					
36	CREMATION				34U⁴					
37	O O				22B5 37J²'			50		J
38	36 75 12 W N O	G		891		43	16		
39	84 42 36		G		225 55T¹⁵ 85E⁷K²					J
40	96 D1 42 E UP O	PIT		14R² 22C²,23V² 46N 85J¹³		265			
41	85 36 50 S E O	L		43E³ 89J6		146			
42	18 84 6		G		89H²K 130,151,280-1					
43	O		R		19E¹ 89H²K					
44	21 70 24 SW SE O	G		35C¹,4>H³,51W² 89F,J6					
45	18 78 18 SW UP O	G	XV	12G⁶ 89J6,L⁵H		172	17,25		L
46	100 DIAM 54		PIT		6C³,15L⁵,17V⁵27J³14¹⁹ 53G 91A⁵					
47	48 90 12 S		G	XVIII	89Q³,6,J,J6 72-3	34,44	22,27,31	+	L
48	20 72 27 W UP O	G		89M		19			E

F. P.

NO.	TOMB N.E.D.	BODY H. F. DIST	TYPE	DYN.	POTTERY				S SCARABS	M METAL	R STONE	B BONE &c	MUS.
1149	50 140 45		C		19 P4					83,130,135, 138	41		
50	90 18 36 NE		L		10 H4			89 G5, J6,9, L5		159	28		J
51	CREMATION					32 D' 53 J							
52	72 20 15 NE W O		G						174, 184	28 178		100·7	J
53	CREMATION					32 Q2						+	
54	22 60 10 SW		Q	XVI	6 N3	38 H'		89 K2					
55	12 62 12 SW		G					89 H', J5,9 K5					
56	18 80 24		G			51 P8					42, 43		A
57	60 35 24		G			68 A5				217	26		
58	64 22 16		G	XVI	6 N3, 10 E2	43 F4 59 G8 66 H3, 68 A							
59	⊕ S UP O									193-4			
60	CREMATION					34 U2							
61	72 18 35		L			51 P3 68 A3							
62	SHERDS IN RUBBISH		PIT		6 C, 10, 19 F, M2 23,'2 K5,7 28 A', 51 P6 60 Q		89 A 91 B'						
63	84-108×120		G		31 L, Y'9	74 O'1'4'		9 A'	74				L
64	⊕ O				12 G4 31 H2	74 K3							J
65	20 70 18		L	XV		51 P3			75-80	13	34		L
66	57 66 PLAN		C	XIX	3 A2, C, 4 J, 12 G3, 13 H2　43 F3 51 E4 Q4,6, 64 R4,5,6 75 N9 85 R9 89 H1-8 91 J4				81-101	20-1, 23, 84, 245	35-40, 49	{17,18,33 {68-72 119-26 108, 126	jn
68	36 60 10 S UP O		G						172, 185-6			177	
69	15 70 6 SW UP O		G			47 H6							
1170	13 54 SW UP O		G						102				J
	PALACE				YARD CEMETERY								
1401	40 74 60 S N O		PIT		21 X2 28 P3			PLAN					L
4	85 75				43 F4 55 D4			P					J
5	76 100 40				20 U 35 R2 37 J8	76 X4		P					M
6	50 70 SE SW Q		X-XI		23 J' 25 G', 35 R, 38 C', 43 D6 51 G3-4,'8, 60 M5 N5,		P	103-4	202		+	L
7	35 45				23 K7'	60 M5		P					
8					20 T, 21 F, 35 R 43 E7 56 E2								O
9	65 72 NW SE NE E O		X-XI		21 M9, 25 G',5, 38 B2 43 E4,5, 51 G3 60 M4,5,'N		P		203			L
10A	E N O							P					J
10B	E N O								106	204-5			J
10C	N UP				26 C2, 34 B9, 43 E5	60 M6			105	206			J
11	S W				1 M2, 25 E4	51 Y		P					L
12	S N O				28 P5	51 Y2 68 T							L
13	SE W O				25 G5 34 Z9			P					L
14					25 D' 35 R2 51 B5								M
16	N S O				21 D			IN MU		14 42	7		F
17	S N				21 D 43 E4 51 Y			P		74-5			L
18	SE UP				21 V 28 P5 34 B8'			P					F
19	SE UP				20 U, 21 M9 51 Y			P					L
20	SE N				22 N2, 25 G5' 43 E, 51 B5 60 Q13			P					O
21	W N				21 X2 43 E4 51 Y			P					
22	E N				35 R2					85			
23	E N				21 M3 43 E5 51 Y								
24	E SW				25 G5 43 E6 51 G3 60 M4								
1450								P	120-1	1-10			

WEIGHTS

P E Y E M						
5742	HAEMAT I	8	459·6	4	114·8	
3	"	21	61·0	½	122·0	
D A R I C						
4	SAND ST	652	3844·0	30	128·1	MA 1152
5	LIMES T	78	3960·4	30	132·0	PL 956
6	"	806	975·2	6	132·1	
7	SILICEOUS	653	26438·	200	132·2	NADY
S T A T E R						
8	HAEMAT I	493	67·9	½	135·8	
9	LIMES TN	476	685·4	5	137·1	GERAR

Q E D E T						
5750	HAEMAT I	875	694·6	5	138·9	
1	GOLD ARMLETS	696		5	139·2	
2	LIMES T	915	698·7	5	139·7	O E 1067
3	HAEMAT I	49	707·2	5	141·5	J
4	"	499	35·5	¼	142·0	
5	CARNEL N	498	286·9	2	143·4	J
6	SILICEOUS	806	718·85	5	143·7	
7	HAEMAT T	499	18·1	⅛	144·8	
8	GOLD EARRINGS		291·2	2	145·6	
8A	LIMES T	9	1471·5	10	147·2	MO 1080

K H O R I N E					
9	GOLD RING		170·3	1	170·3
5760	" TOGGLE		172·3	1	172·3
1	" EARRING RIBB3		57·8	⅓	175·4
2	" TOGGLE		89·1	½	178·2
3	HAEMAT I	487	90·5	½	181·0
4	"	802	90·8	½	181·6
5	BASALT	821	910·8	5	182·1
6	PORPHYRY	149	187·1	1	187·1

BEQA, AEGINETAN						
5767	LIMES TN	923	5710	1/16	913 b	NH 1060
8	LEAD	605	572·2	1/16	9155	OTAWJ
9	GOLD RING		49·3	¼	197·2	
5770	LIMES TN	917	805·0	4	201·2	OF 976
1	HAEMAT T	397	203·6	1	203·6	
2	MARBLE + PB	11	1664·4	8	208·0	1070
3	LIMES N	9	1664·8	8	208·1	PF 1095

SELA, PHOENICIAN						
4	HAEMAT T	50	107·1	½	214·2	
5	LIMES TN	653	21722·	100	217·2	MF 1144
6	HAEMAT I	493	109·1	½	218·2	
7	BASALT	12	5503·0	25	220·0	
8	SHELLY LIMES TN	64	4419	20	220·9	

5767, 5972 an iron handle may be missing.

NO.	TOMB N.E.D.	BODY H F Dist	TYPE	DYN.	POTTERY	S SCARABS	M METAL	R STONE	B BONE&c	MUS.
1501	⊕		G		34Z7,38A1					I
2	18 72 10 S W O		G		31H 43F 68A2	107	29,41,218-9,246			J
3	15 43 9		G		32D4,34Z7 64A4,68A3					J
4	⊕ BURNT		PIT		38O7		11-12 293-4	45-8		L
5	⊕		R		23G3 89H5					
6	⊕ SW N		R		34E4 85,19 89K5					
7	16 69 10 SW		S		89H3		16	12,13		J
8	18 51 8		S		43H6 89H2					
9	12 84 8 SW NW		S	AK III	19E1 43H3,51V2 69E2 89H1	108				O
10	⊕		R	T.III	89K8	109,110				J
12	⊕		G		36G6,38O6,43E5 74O8"					
13	O		PIT		23K21' 38D 38S2		{27 {77,136-7,150-7			L
14	50 106 72 SW PLAN		G	XVIII	12Q,19E2,O2,23K16,22' 31D' 51V2 64R5 85N4,Q19,91S,V		{160, as 172	as 38	26-31	L
15	⊕				36G5H3,19E2 43H4					
16	35 60 33 E N O		SL				55			H
17	42 60 54 E N O		SL		30F4,33M4		60			O
18	O				9E,E2,F 30G1,6					J
19	O				4E,H,H2 68A2		27			L
20	60 60 42 E N O		PIT		30F5					
21	72 48 60 S E O		G				63			M
22	48 75 54		S		30J7					
23	54 64 16				30F5					
24	45 57 30		S		30F7					
25	32 51 30 SE		S		30F7					
26	51 63 48 SE ME		S				47			J
27	36 81 SE NE		G				49			N
28	90 70 E N		S		30G2					
30	48 70 55 SE NE O		SL		30F7		62			G
31	54 66 30 SE NE		G				57			N
32	40 63 33 E N O		SL				48	RING		J
33	36 48 36		SL						128 129	
34	50 60 48 S E		S		30F7,33M7'		67			J
35	39 69 42 E N O		G				51			R
37	39 78 33 E N O		SL				61			L
38	36 75 42 E N		SL		30F5		59			J
39	160 155 100 E N		PIT				56			L
40	O				30F8					
41	50 80 48 E S		G		30J2					
42	72 96 30 E N O		S		30F7		66			L
43	78 50 30		S	XV	6N3 43A2,C4,53R3		70			J
44	60 48 36 E N Q		SL				65			H
45	40 55 42 E N O		SL		30F8		58			E
46	48 84 42 E N O		S				50		130	L M
47	72 36 30 E N O		S		30F9					
48	48 50 50 E N O		G		30F4					
49	51 72 30		SC		30F6					
50	78 84 90 E S O		G		4H,H2 30J6					
51	63 84 45 E N O		G				53			G
52	33 66 24 E N O		SC				68			J
53	80 54 57 E N O				30F0					
54	50 64 30		SC		30F4					
55	38 69 30		S		30J8					
56	108 51 30 E N		S		30F4					
57	36 54 36		S		30J8					
58	36 60 30 E?		SC		30J4					
59	40 56 20 E S O		SC		30J9					
60	43 67 23 E S O		SC		30J4					
62	55 100 31 E S O		SC		30J4					
64	36 39 20 E N O		SC		69L2					
65	74 76 28 E N O		SC		30G0'		64			G
66	50 80 24 E N O		SC		30G0				+ 131	
67	66/56 52/36 28 E S O		SC							
69	50 54 30 E N O		SC		30F8		52			L
70	24 60 18		S				54			W
71	O				23E10 35P5					
72	54 40 28 E S O									
73	O RUBBISH		PIT		15W1 30A,J2,N2,31Q2,32E					
74	40 DIAM 230				SHERDS					
75	48 40 400				,,					

F.P.

For EU product safety concerns, contact us at Calle de José Abascal, 56–1°,
28003 Madrid, Spain or eugpsr@cambridge.org.

www.ingramcontent.com/pod-product-compliance
Ingram Content Group UK Ltd.
Pitfield, Milton Keynes, MK11 3LW, UK
UKHW051028150625
459647UK00023B/2855